Lord of Life
King of the Universe
Master of Everything

42 days leading up to the coming of Christ

Major Stephen M. Kelly

Copyright © 2023 by The Salvation Army USA Southern Territory

All rights reserved. This book or any portion thereof may not be reproduced or used in any manner whatsoever without express written permission of the publisher except for the use of brief quotations in a book review.

Unless otherwise indicated, all Scripture quotations are taken from the Holy Bible, New Living Translation, copyright © 1996, 2004, 2015 by Tyndale House Foundation. Used by permission of Tyndale House Publishers, Inc., Carol Stream, Illinois 60188. All rights reserved.

Quotations from the Apocrypha are taken from the New Revised Standard Version Bible: Anglicised Catholic Edition, copyright © 1989, 1993, 1995 the Division of Christian Education of the National Council of the Churches of Christ in the United States of America. Used by permission. All rights reserved.

Quotations from the works of Josephus are taken from the website of the Center for Judaic Studies—www.cojs.org

For information write:

The Salvation Army
USA Southern Territory
Literary Council
1424 Northeast Expressway
Atlanta, GA 30329

ISBN: 978-0-86544-097-5

Printed in the United States of America

Table of Contents

Foreword	Commissioner William Francis	v
	The Genealogy of Jesus the Messiah	vii
November 14	Introduction	1
November 15	Abraham	5
November 16	Isaac	7
November 17	Jacob	9
November 18	Judah	11
November 19	Perez	13
November 20	Hezron	15
November 21	Ram	17
November 22	Amminadab	19
November 23	Nahshon	21
November 24	Salmon	23
November 25	Boaz	25
November 26	Obed	27
November 27	Jesse	29
November 28	David	31
November 29	Solomon	33
November 30	Rehoboam	35
December 1	Abijah	37
December 2	Asa	39
December 3	Jehoshaphat	41

December 4	Jehoram	43
December 5	Uzziah	45
December 6	Jotham	47
December 7	Ahaz	49
December 8	Hezekiah	51
December 9	Manasseh	53
December 10	Amon	55
December 11	Josiah	57
December 12	Jehoiachin and his brothers	59
December 13	Shealtiel	61
December 14	Zerubbabel	63
December 15	Abiud	67
December 16	Eliakim	69
December 17	Azor	73
December 18	Zadok	75
December 19	Akim	77
December 20	Elihud	79
December 21	Eleazar	83
December 22	Matthan	87
December 23	Jacob	89
December 24	Joseph	91
December 25	Jesus	93
	About the author	95

Foreword

COMMISSIONER WILLIAM FRANCIS

From dull genealogy to heightened truth! Through 42 days of devotional reflection, Major Stephen Kelly guides us on a surprisingly interesting, powerful discovery of truth from the oft maligned study of biblical genealogy. He proves that the consideration of genealogy can be a fascinating, thought provoking mental and spiritual journey, especially when tracing the lineage of Jesus.

Even steadfast students of the Bible have tended to skim over the mysterious, complicated, and often difficult-to-pronounce lineages scattered throughout Scripture. Genealogies, however, provide remarkable insight into biblical truth. The genealogies listed in Genesis, Numbers, Chronicles, Ezra, Nehemiah, as well as New Testament listings of Jesus' lineage in Matthew and Luke, serve as the underpinnings of biblical truth.

Throughout the history of the Israelite nation, geneologies were the key, primary sources of information. For example, when Artaxerxes permitted his cupbearer, Nehemiah, to return to Jerusalem for the purpose of rebuilding the city in 445 BC, Nehemiah's first act was to consult the genealogical record – "Then my God put it into my heart to assemble the nobles and the officials and the people to be enrolled by genealogy. And I found the book of the genealogy of those who came up at the first ...." (Nehemiah 7:5ff).

My esteemed colleague and friend, Major Stephen Kelly, has provided a concise, yet inclusive, compelling study of the Jesus' ancestry. He does so through his signature laid-back, conversational style based on solid scholarship.

In preparation for the study, why is it important affirm why genealogical passages are valuable to Bible study? I suggest five reasons:

1) They corroborate the reliability of the Bible. The genealogical record provides a sturdy superstructure holding the biblical history, diverse cultures, and varied narratives together.

2) They highlight the importance of family to God, as well as the sundry writers of Scripture.

3) Genealogies were essential in verifying who could serve in specialized religious roles. For example, it was the Levites who served in the Tabernacle and later in the Jerusalem Temple. It was also vital in documenting the descendants of Aaron who bore the important responsibility of high priest.

4) Genealogies reveal that God used a wide diversity of individuals throughout history to conduct His divine will. He chose individuals from the least to the greatest; from the highly qualified to the markedly unqualified.

5) Crucially, biblical genealogy corroborates biblical prophecy. Jesus was a Jew from the tribe of Judah and a descendant of Abraham and David.

Major Stephen Kelly brings to life the 41 ancestors of Jesus. Just as all family trees contains a unique assortment of ancestors, so it was with Jesus' lineage. This list includes Judah, the son of Jacob, who unintentionally slept with Tamar, his daughter-in-law. Rahab was a prostitute. Ruth was a pagan Moabite woman. David, "a man after God's own heart" (1 Samuel 13:14; Acts 13:22), committed murder and adultery. Jesus' earthly family tree varied in wisdom, leadership, and integrity, but were all used by God.

I highly recommend this fresh look at the biblical personalities whom God choose as the human progenitures His Son… "the King of Kings and Lord of Lords" (Revelation 19:16).

William W. Francis
Commissioner

The Genealogy of Jesus the Messiah

This is a record of the ancestors of Jesus the Messiah, a descendant of David and of Abraham:

2 Abraham was the father of Isaac.
Isaac was the father of Jacob.
Jacob was the father of Judah and his brothers.

3 Judah was the father of Perez and Zerah (whose mother was Tamar).
Perez was the father of Hezron.
Hezron was the father of Ram.

4 Ram was the father of Amminadab.
Amminadab was the father of Nahshon.
Nahshon was the father of Salmon.

5 Salmon was the father of Boaz (whose mother was Rahab).
Boaz was the father of Obed (whose mother was Ruth).
Obed was the father of Jesse.

6 Jesse was the father of King David.
David was the father of Solomon (whose mother was Bathsheba, the widow of Uriah).

7 Solomon was the father of Rehoboam.
Rehoboam was the father of Abijah.
Abijah was the father of Asa.

8 Asa was the father of Jehoshaphat.
Jehoshaphat was the father of Jehoram.
Jehoram was the father of Uzziah.

9 Uzziah was the father of Jotham.
Jotham was the father of Ahaz.
Ahaz was the father of Hezekiah.

10   Hezekiah was the father of Manasseh.
     Manasseh was the father of Amon.
     Amon was the father of Josiah.

11   Josiah was the father of Jehoiachin and his brothers
     (born at the time of the exile to Babylon).

12   After the Babylonian exile:
     Jehoiachin was the father of Shealtiel.
     Shealtiel was the father of Zerubbabel.

13   Zerubbabel was the father of Abiud.
     Abiud was the father of Eliakim.
     Eliakim was the father of Azor.

14   Azor was the father of Zadok.
     Zadok was the father of Akim.
     Akim was the father of Eliud.

15   Eliud was the father of Eleazar.
     Eleazar was the father of Matthan.
     Matthan was the father of Jacob.

16   Jacob was the father of Joseph, the husband of Mary.
     Mary gave birth to Jesus, who is called the Messiah.

17   All those listed above include fourteen generations from Abraham to David, fourteen from David to the Babylonian exile, and fourteen from the Babylonian exile to the Messiah.

Matthew 1:1-17, New Living Translation

November 14

INTRODUCTION

> *This is a record of the ancestors of Jesus the Messiah, a descendant of David and of Abraham:*

Matthew begins his gospel by tracing the family heritage of Jesus Christ. For most people, reading a genealogy couldn't be duller, unless it's their own. I doubt Matthew 1:1-17 gets read in church very often, and I think a lot of people just skip this passage to get to "the good stuff."

Many an unbeliever has been handed a New Testament with no direction of what to read first, and so they start on page 1 - and get no further. I wish the Council of Rome that set the canon of Scripture had put either the book of Mark or John first for this reason.

But 2 Timothy 3:16-17 assures us that "All Scripture is God-breathed and is useful for teaching, rebuking, correcting and training in righteousness, so that the servant of God may be thoroughly equipped for every good work." *All Scripture* includes the genealogies, here in Matthew as well as in Luke, Genesis and the books of Chronicles, and others. The genealogies are useful for teaching, rebuking, and so forth. They're there for a reason!

In retirement, my father, Colonel Paul Kelly, took a great interest in genealogy, tracing our family heritage back to the mid 800's AD. He made cousin connections to numerous British kings and U.S. presidents. There was even an election year (2004) where we were related to both candidates! I have an ancestor who was a signer on the first colonial charter that promised freedom of religion (Rhode Island, 1663).

Recently my wife had a *23 and Me* genetic test and found that not only did she have the expected Irish, Scottish and German heritage, but surprisingly had a connection to the Congo as well.

People are often fascinated to find out where their family came from, making connections to faraway places and the stories of earlier times.

As we look at the genealogy of Christ as recorded in Matthew, it will take us on a journey to the stories of times leading up to His arrival. We'll see the prophecies predicting His coming in the context of the times they were heard.

Matthew was likely a numbers guy. Before his calling by Christ, he was a tax collector, so he had to know the accounting methods of his day. Pliny the Elder, a Roman historian in the first century, records that an early system of double-entry accounting was in place in that era. Since I've worked in the finance and audit departments, Matthew's someone I can relate to. He understood debits and credits along with the importance of having your records in good order. I can imagine him and Zacchaeus discussing the nuances of support service policy[1]. Given Matthew's background, it is funny how Judas got custody of the petty cash instead of the former tax accountant. (See John 12:6.)

Not surprisingly, this numbers guy, Matthew, makes use of a literary memorization tactic popular in his day by breaking his genealogy into groups. On a couple of occasions, he compresses a couple of generations to make it fit his model of three groups of fourteen. These numbers have great biblical significance.

First, fourteen is twice seven, and is the number of days it takes for a new moon to become full. Older translations of the Bible often use the phrase, "in the fullness of days," to indicate that an event is bringing history to a climax. More modern translations say, "when the time came." (See Galatians 4:4 and Ephesians 1:10)

Three, of course, points to the Holy Trinity of God.

And three times 14 is 42, which is not "the answer to life, the universe and everything," as made famous by Douglas Adams, but is actually a more obscure biblical number. Forty-two is six (the biblical number for man, created on the sixth day) times

---

[1] Support service is the means whereby Salvation Army field and headquarters locations calculate the fees to the next level of headquarters covering a wide variety of services.

seven (the biblical number for completeness or wholeness). So, 42 points to Jesus as the complete, whole man, what Adam should have been but fell short.

Revelation 11:2 says that Gentiles "will trample on the holy city for 42 months" which, according to premillennial theology, is the midpoint of the seven-year tribulation period and the time when Antichrist will break his covenant. In the times leading up to Christ's coming, the holy city had successively been trampled by invasions of Babylonians (Nebuchadnezzar), Persians (Xerxes), Greeks (Alexander), and Romans (Pompey). Interestingly, 42 x 14 gives you 588, which is about the number of years from the fall of Jerusalem under Nebuchadnezzar, when the Gentiles began their "trampling," to the coming of Christ.

Forty-two is the number of stopping places recorded in Numbers for the Israelites leaving Egypt heading to the Promised Land.

Here's an odd fact. Hebrew scrolls of the Torah have 42 lines of text per page. The scribes felt the number was significant due to the places in Numbers. This was repeated when the Gutenberg Bible was first printed with 42 lines of text per page, following the pattern of the Latin Vulgate translation which did the same.

The point is, for whatever reason, Matthew chose to use 42 as an outline structure for his genealogy from Abraham to Christ. I'm sure he wasn't thinking of Elisha's bears (See 2 Kings 2:23-24). He felt this structure was significant in pointing us to Christ.

As we work through his framework leading into Advent, may we, too, be pointed to the coming Messiah.

November 15

ABRAHAM

The Messiah Who blesses the world

Abraham was the father of Isaac,

Abram (later Abraham) received a number of promises when God called him to leave his home country and go to a land that God would show him (See Genesis 12). Among them were:
- I will make you a blessing to others;
- All families on earth will be blessed through you;
- I will give this land to your descendants.

This is Abraham's first hint that God was going to give him a child, even though he was 75 years old by this time and he and his wife had never been able to have children. That would have to change to have descendants. There were also promises of being great and famous, of God giving protection and cursing those who cursed Abraham. Life's going to treat you well, Abraham.

God delights in blessing His children with good things. But there's always a purpose, and it's not just so we can have good things and keep them to ourselves. Second Corinthians 1:3-4 says that God comforts us, not so we'd be comfortable, but so we can turn around and comfort other people in need of that same comfort.

I know a couple who lost a teenage child in a car accident. This is a terrible wound that never really goes away, but God has provided great healing over the years. They in turn participate in a ministry to other people who have lost children, passing on what God has done for them in a way that only they can.

Abraham was told from the beginning that the blessings he was to receive had a future purpose of blessing others—in fact, the whole world, and that it was connected to his having descendants. Here are hints of the coming of Jesus.

Later, Abraham saw how concerned God was with the cities of Sodom and Gomorrah, where sin had metastasized into complete depravity. His nephew, Lot, was foolishly in the middle of the moral carnage, trying to raise his family in a city that had terribly lost its way. Abraham saw firsthand that his Lord is a God who rescues people from sin, pulling them out of the mess even though they voluntarily got into it. He could have left Lot and his family to die along with the rest of the city that had less than ten righteous people in it, but the rescuing God wouldn't do that. Could rescuing from sin be part of the plan to bless the nations through Abraham's descendants?

In fact, Lot was rescued from Sodom *twice:* first in battle through Abraham and Lot went right back to Sodom only to be supernaturally rescued by God's angels. This God of Abraham is relentless in trying to save us.

Abraham learned that the God who saves wanted to bless the whole world through his descendants. A closer look at the promise in Genesis 12:7 shows that the word translated *descendants*, לְזַרְעֲךָ (lə·zar·ʽă·ḵā) is constructed as a singular male noun. The blessings wouldn't come through Abraham's descendants as a group, but specifically through a particular male descendant. The Savior is on His way.

Consider: If you're a follower of Jesus, think of ways that you, too, can bless the world around you. What is Jesus asking you to do to take His blessing to you and pass it on to others?

November 16

ISAAC

The Messiah Who is the Lamb of God

Isaac the father of Jacob,

Isaac is in this strange position of being *actually* the second-born but *legally* firstborn because of Abraham's foolish attempt to bring about God's promise through Hagar his servant, rather than through his wife, Sarah. Ishmael's birth brought a whole heap of regret and trouble into Abraham's household. But God made clear His intent that His promises were to come through Isaac, to the point of referring to Isaac as "your son, your *only* son, whom you love…" (Genesis 22:2), and twice more in that same chapter. Similar language appears at Jesus' baptism when God calls Him "My Son, whom I love" (Matthew 3:17 NIV).

Jesus, too, is in an odd position in terms of birth order. Colossians 1:15 (NIV) calls Jesus the "firstborn over all creation." Modern translations sadly leave out the word, "begotten," from John 3:16, especially given all the energy early church councils expended trying to grapple with the idea of how Jesus could be both eternal and yet be begotten by the Father. Today we kind of just gloss over the doctrinal importance of Jesus' "begottenness."

Yet while Jesus is firstborn and leads a long train of adopted sons and daughters in God's family, in another sense He's second born. First Corinthians 15:45 calls Him the Second Adam. He's the one who succeeded where the first Adam failed – in giving perfect obedience to God. Where Adam 1.0 brought sin into the world, Adam 2.0 brought holiness. This is all part of the mystery of how Jesus can be both "truly and properly God" (firstborn) and "truly and properly man" (second born). He's not 50% divine and 50% human. He's 100% of both.

That Genesis 22:2 reference doesn't stop with identifying Isaac as Abraham's only, beloved son. This is where Abraham is commanded to take Isaac to Mount Moriah, the future site of Jerusalem, to sacrifice him there. One wonders what's going through Abraham's head at this point, since Isaac's not going to have any descendants if he's dead. How is God going to fulfill His promises with Isaac out of the picture? Hebrews 11:17-19 tells us that Abraham fully expected to go through with the sacrifice but believed that Isaac would be raised from the dead.

At the time, He didn't tell Isaac everything He was thinking. He didn't even tell Isaac the whole story of why they were climbing the mountain in the first place, because Isaac wondered, "We have the fire and the wood…but where is the sheep for the burnt offering?" (Genesis 22:7).

Abraham wisely and prophetically replies, "God himself will provide the lamb for the burnt offering, my son" (Genesis 22:8 NIV). At the last possible moment, God intervenes and stops Abraham from going through with it. A substitute sacrifice is provided, and father and son worship together, rejoicing that they were both still alive.

God didn't ask Abraham to do anything He wasn't willing to do Himself, including offering His Son, His only Son, Whom He loved, as a sacrifice for sin. Only when Jesus came to die at Mount Calvary – only a short distance from Mount Moriah – there was no last-minute reprieve. He was the "The Lamb of God who takes away the sin of the world" (John 1:29).

And so, Abraham's hope that Isaac would rise from the dead was fulfilled by the Substitute Lamb. We all can live with the hope of resurrection in Him as well.

Consider: Since God wouldn't hold back anything for your salvation, including His Only Son, what might you be holding back from Him?

November 17

JACOB

The Messiah Whose promises are personal

Jacob the father of Judah and his brothers,

Jacob is the second-born of a set of twins, after his brother, Esau.

Isaac watched with horror as his eldest married Canaanite women, who led him astray and into idol worship. He was determined that Jacob wouldn't make the same mistake. So, he sent Jacob back to the land Abraham had come from, and where his own wife, Rebekah had come from. Along the way, Jacob stopped at a place he would call, "Beth-El", "house of God." There he had his famous dream (Genesis 28:10-15):

> *As he slept, he dreamed of a stairway that reached from the earth up to heaven. And he saw the angels of God going up and down the stairway.*

John the Baptist, centuries later, brought up this image in John 1:51, where he said of Christ, "I tell you the truth, you will all see heaven open and the angels of God going up and down on the Son of Man…" picturing Jesus Himself as the stairway connecting heaven to earth.

Jacob's dream continued:

> *And all the families of the earth will be blessed through you and your descendants. What's more, I am with you, and I will protect you wherever you go. One day I will bring you back to this land. I will not leave you until I have finished giving you everything I have promised you."*

In some ways, this would seem to be a repeat of the promises given to Abraham and Isaac, and of course, "all the families of the earth will be blessed through you and your descendants" is another reference to the coming of Christ.

In English, if you're talking to a male, you say, "you." If you're talking to a female, you say, "you." There's no distinction. But in Hebrew there is. See the verse again, marked with gender:

> *What's more, I am with you (female), and I will protect you (male) wherever you go. One day I will bring you (male) back to this land. I will not leave you (male) until I have finished giving you (female) everything I have promised..."*

Remember that God had given Jacob a new name, "Israel," and that new name in many ways became synonymous with Jacob's descendants, not just him personally.

God is making personal promises to Jacob (the masculine phrases) and He is also making promises to Israel as a people (the feminine phrases).

So, God promises to Jacob personally that he'll be protected, will return home, and God will not leave him along the way.

But the promise that "I am with you" and the mention that God's not going to quit until He's finished giving everything He promised are given **to Israel as a people**.

You see, Jacob is learning that God's promises of the One who is coming are not pointing out a Savior that will be just for him or his family. Christ is coming for all His people.

"I'm not quitting until it's finished," God says. On the cross, Jesus said it finally was. When He returns, "It is finished," will take on a whole new meaning.

Consider: In what sense do you believe God is with you? Are there any areas of your life where you need to get on God's side instead of expecting Him to be on yours?

November 18

JUDAH

The Messiah from the royal tribe

Judah the father of Perez and Zerah, whose mother was Tamar,

Judah is the fourth-born of Jacob's huge family. You'd think by now we would have gotten the point that while human society seems to favor the firstborn, and even the law of Moses later specified better inheritance rights for the firstborn of a family (Deuteronomy 21:17), God often chooses the not-so-obvious to fulfill His promises.

The biblical narrative gives us little about the life of Judah; the text focuses heavily on his younger brother, Joseph, who was Jacob's all-too-obvious favorite son. But when the jealous brothers hatched a plan to kill Joseph, two brothers tried in different ways to save him. Reuben's plan was to throw him into a cistern, supposedly left to die, but Reuben planned to secretly rescue him. Judah had the idea of saving his life *and* getting rid of him by selling him into slavery. Better than dead, but not by much.

Once Joseph was off to Egypt, Judah grew up, got married and had three children. The eldest, Er, married a woman named Tamar. Er ended up dying without an heir. Tamar, destitute, tricks Judah into thinking she was a prostitute and ends up pregnant by her father-in-law. Yuck.

Years go by, and Joseph has gone from the slave trader's block to the head of Potiphar's household to prison and on to become Pharoah's right-hand man.

Judah, too, has done some growing up.

Famine strikes, and the brothers travel to Egypt to buy food – without Benjamin, Jacob's new favorite once he thought Joseph was dead. In disguise, Pharoah's chief of staff, Joseph, tells them they won't be allowed to return without the little brother.

A considerably more mature Judah takes the lead in convincing the father to let Benjamin go: "Send the boy with me, and we will be on our way. Otherwise, we will all die of starvation—and not only we, but you and our little ones. I personally guarantee his safety. You may hold me responsible if I don't bring him back to you. Then let me bear the blame forever" (Genesis 43:8-9).

Later, Joseph tests his brothers, planting a silver cup in their bags of food and then accusing them of stealing. Judah now takes a leadership position, personally accepting the blame for the theft to protect his little brother -- everything he *should* have done for Joseph but didn't (Genesis 44:16-34).

Joseph sees Judah isn't the same man who sold his brother into slavery. He's no longer the jealous, angry, selfish man he once was.

Jacob, too, has seen how Judah has changed. Doubtless once he heard Joseph was still alive, the whole story came out, and he knew Judah had been the one with the slavery idea. But he became Benjamin's protector. He learned. He grew.

When Jacob was on his deathbed, he gave each of his sons his blessing. This was Judah's:

> *"The scepter will not depart from Judah, nor the ruler's staff from his descendants, until the coming of the one to whom it belongs, the one whom all nations will honor."*

Judah, fourth-born betrayer of Dad's favorite, is declared to be the head of the royal family. He's earned his place of leadership by putting his own life on the line to save someone else.

So, too, the King of kings is to be called that not because of His royal lineage, but because He would "give His life as a ransom for many." (Matthew 20:28)

One day, Jacob says, "Someone will come from Judah's line. The scepter belongs to Him. And all nations will honor Him."

Consider: How have you grown since becoming a believer? Are you doing better at living up to the name of Christ than you did at first?

November 19

Perez

The Messiah with billions of children

Perez the father of Hezron,

Perez was born before the family packed up and moved to Egypt, the product of Judah's liaison with his daughter-in-law, one of a set of twins. Perez probably spent most of his adult life in Goshen.

While in Egypt, all the Israelites multiplied remarkably (Exodus 1:7). This did not attract the concern of Pharaoh right away. In the short term, due to Joseph's influence, the Israelites enjoyed the favor of Egypt's leadership. They had a great piece of land in which to settle down, build homes, and enlarge their flocks and other wealth. The Egyptians, with their idol worship and foreign practices, and disliking shepherds, kept their distance, limiting their influence on the growing tribes of Israel.

Perez was particularly blessed, though we don't know exactly how many children and grandchildren he had. But generations later, in Ruth 4:12, there is a blessing wishing Boaz and Ruth to have many children **like Perez did.**

His many children contributed to the fact that, when the Exodus occurred, his tribe of Judah added more in population than any other tribe (see Numbers 26). This trend for Judah to have a large population continued into the Promised Land, where they became the dominant tribe and give their tribal name to the southern kingdom after the civil war.

This brings us to the question of the descendants of Jesus. For centuries, people from the Merovingian dynasty of France to Dan Brown (*The Da Vinci Code*) have tried to suggest that Jesus married Mary Magdalene and had physical descendants by her. **The Bible gives no support whatsoever to this fantasy.** In fact, the Bible specifically contradicts it in Isaiah 53:8. Speaking of Jesus' crucifixion, the prophet says, "Unjustly condemned, he was led away. No one cared that **he died without descendants**, that his life was cut short in midstream." In Middle Eastern culture, it was considered a horrible tragedy for someone to die before having children.

And yet in another way, Jesus ended up being more prolific than Perez.

John 1:12-13 says, "But to all who believed him and accepted him, he gave the right to become children of God. They are reborn—not with a physical birth resulting from human passion or plan, but a birth that comes from God."

You see, it wasn't God's plan that Jesus have descendants in the physical sense "resulting from human passion or plan" but that His family grew through faith in Him.

Hebrews 2:10 tells us, "God, for whom and through whom everything was made, chose to bring many children into glory. And it was only right that he should make Jesus, through his suffering, a perfect leader, fit to bring them into their salvation."

"See how very much our Father loves us, for he calls us his children, and that is what we are!" (1 John 3:1).

We are His many, many children, now numbering in the billions.

Beat that, Perez.

Consider: Bearing fruit implies you're planting seeds for the next generation of believers. Are you reproducing your faith in others?

November 20

HEZRON

The Messiah Who uses tribulation

Hezron the father of Ram,

Hezron was a member of the generation where things started to go downhill for Israel's family. "Eventually, a new king came to power in Egypt who knew nothing about Joseph or what he had done" (Exodus 1:8).

How does that happen? Certainly, the Israelites didn't forget Joseph. And the Egyptian dynasties had impeccable recordkeepers. The most likely reason that Joseph was forgotten was that it became politically necessary to forget him. Those who had control of the records made the "necessary" updates to reflect the new political realities.

After all, if the pharaohs wanted to consider themselves "gods" and expected everyone to go along with it, a story about a pharaoh needing help from a Hebrew just didn't go over very well. As George Orwell put it in *1984,* "Who controls the past controls the future. Who controls the present controls the past."

The new pharaoh felt threatened by the rapidly multiplying Israelites, fearing they could turn on him in case of war. So, he enslaved them, setting up the circumstances that led to the Exodus.

Perez prosperity is inevitably followed by Hezron tribulation. Good times never are permanent. Society forgets the great stories and truths of the past, or intentionally rewrites history so the great stories become bad. Saviors can be recast as oppressors —if they're remembered at all.

Jesus warned us that "Here on earth you will have many trials and sorrows." (John 16:33). In fact, being a follower of Jesus more often than not means trouble, not prosperity. In America, most Christians are blissfully ignorant of the persecution suffered by fellow believers around the world. We think we've got it bad when we're labeled as whatever-phobes and bigots for not going along with the flavor-of-the-month in moral decay, while in other places Christians suffer discrimination, imprisonment, rape, having children taken away and even death for following Christ.

In Hezron's day, "…the more the Egyptians oppressed them, the more the Israelites multiplied and spread" (Exodus 1:12). After warning us we'd have trials and sorrows, Jesus adds, "But take heart, because I have overcome the world." And because He overcomes, we overcome. Romans 8:37 tells us, "No, despite all these things, overwhelming victory is ours through Christ, who loved us."

Doesn't mean it's easy when you're going through it. Tertullian, one of the early church fathers, wrote that "The blood of the martyrs is the seed of the church," because it seems that the church grows *faster* when it's under persecution.

Jesus won't tolerate a lukewarm church (Revelation 3:16). So sometimes He turns up the heat.

Consider: Do you try to find out about the persecuted church around the world and pray for your brothers and sisters who suffer? Do you find yourself complaining too much in the light of what they go through?

November 21

RAM

The Messiah Who delivers from sin

Ram the father of Amminadab,

Ram was of the generation that saw the birth of Moses, though Moses wasn't recognized as the nation's deliverer until the next generation, aged 80. Ram's generation was among those pictured in the song, "Deliver Us" from *The Prince of Egypt,* which like its predecessor *The Ten Commandments* tries to capture the desperate mood of the people of Ram's day. While both films show the horrors of slavery under Egypt, the more recent film does so with a more Jewish – and thus more historically accurate – feel.

As the years dragged on, the people must have wondered if God was listening. When God appears at the burning bush, He tells Moses, "I have certainly seen the oppression of my people in Egypt. I have heard their cries of distress because of their harsh slave drivers. Yes, I am aware of their suffering…Look! The cry of the people of Israel has reached me, and I have seen how harshly the Egyptians abuse them" (Exodus 3:7,9).

We all have become slaves to sin simply by being human. But we've forged our own chains by the sinful choices we make. The condition of sin and the actions of sin are linked, and there's no escape without a Savior. Sin is a very harsh taskmaster, at its worst stripping souls of their humanity and laying waste to countless lives. Day by day it seems new ways to ruin people are being thought up.

Watch how short a time it is between a child learning to talk and learning to lie, and then try to tell me there's no such thing as "original sin" pulling us all down.

Years later, Moses promised that:

> *"The Lord your God will raise up for you a prophet like me from among your fellow Israelites. You must listen to him. …I will raise up a prophet like you from among their fellow Israelites. I will put my words in his mouth, and he will tell the people everything I command him. I will personally deal with anyone who will not listen to the messages the prophet proclaims on my behalf. (Deuteronomy 18:15-19)*

Jesus came saying, "I don't speak on my own authority. The Father who sent me has commanded me what to say and how to say it" (John 12:49).

As the Deliverer, Jesus fulfilled the prophecy of Isaiah 61:1-3:

> *"The Spirit of the Sovereign Lord is upon me, for the Lord has anointed me to bring good news to the poor. He has sent me to comfort the brokenhearted and to proclaim that captives will be released and prisoners will be freed. He has sent me to tell those who mourn that the time of the Lord's favor has come, and with it, the day of God's anger against their enemies.*
>
> *To all who mourn in Israel, he will give a crown of beauty for ashes, a joyous blessing instead of mourning, festive praise instead of despair…*

Like Moses, He led His people out of bondage and on to a new place of blessing.

Both Jesus and Moses called themselves "humble" (Numbers 12:3; Matthew 11:29).

Both Jesus and Moses performed incredible miracles.

Both referred to themselves as a "shepherd" (Exodus 4:2; John 10:11).

But only One laid down His life for the sheep.

Consider: How can you comfort the brokenhearted, proclaim freedom for captives, reach the mourning with the good news of God's favor? How can you be Jesus to a hurting world?

November 22

AMMINADAB

The Messiah Who expects faithfulness

Amminadab the father of Nahshon,

Amminadab was among the generation that experienced the events of the Exodus.

The ever-increasing pressure from an angry pharaoh.

Blood. Frogs. Gnats. Flies. Disease. Boils. Hail. Locusts. Darkness.

And then the Passover. The night of horrors that opened the way to go home.

The chase through the desert and the parting of the Red Sea. Egyptians lying dead on the shore.

Water from a rock. Manna. Quail. Fire and cloud.

Over and over and over God shows His mighty hand—and the people rebel anyway.

Amminadab has reason to be more loyal than his comrades. He's Aaron's father-in-law. According to Exodus 6:23, "Aaron married Elisheba, the daughter of Amminadab and sister of Nahshon, and she gave birth to his sons, Nadab, Abihu, Eleazar, and Ithamar." He's right in the middle of everything that's going on. Amminadab's got a front-row seat watching his son-in-law be Moses' spokesman.

It's likely he knew Moses pretty well, since he and Aaron were virtually inseparable except when it came to mountain climbing.

But for all he's seen, for all he's heard, for all he's experienced firsthand, Amminadab won't make it to the Land of Promise.

See, Amminadab had a cousin named Caleb. And Caleb was among the twelve who explored Canaan, and one of only two who came back and said, "Let's go at once to take the land; We can certainly conquer it!" (Numbers 13:30)

Unfortunately, Caleb (and Joshua) didn't win the day. They were overruled.

> *Then the whole community began weeping aloud, and they cried all night. Their voices rose in a great chorus of protest against Moses and Aaron. "If only we had died in Egypt, or even here in the wilderness!" they complained. "Why is the Lord taking us to this country only to have us die in battle? Our wives and our little ones will be carried off as plunder! Wouldn't it be better for us to return to Egypt?" Then they plotted among themselves, "Let's choose a new leader and go back to Egypt!" Numbers 14:1-4*

Amminadab would have been among the rebels. After all he'd seen and been through, he couldn't muster up the faith to believe that the same God who conquered the Egyptians could also conquer the Canaanites. He turned on his own son-in-law, or at the very least kept his mouth shut and didn't publicly side with Caleb and Joshua.

Jesus had the same problem with His disciples. Again and again, He asked them, "Where is your faith?" (Matthew 14:31; Matthew 17:17; Mark 4:40; Mark 16:14; Luke 24:25; John 12:37).

And it's funny, even after the disciples saw miracle after miracle, they still had faith issues.

We might be tempted to think, "Those idiot Israelites! Those idiot disciples! How could they not have faith after all they'd seen?"

But then again, we do the same thing. God gets us through something big in our lives, maybe even miraculously, but when the next crisis comes, we wonder. All those past experiences somehow fade in the face of what we're facing today.

But here's the thing. While Jesus longs for us to have more faith, He doesn't give up on us. He didn't give up on the people of Israel, although it would be another generation that entered the Land of Promise; He didn't give up on His disciples. And He doesn't give up on us.

Second Timothy 2:13 tells us "If we are unfaithful, he remains faithful, for he cannot deny who he is."

Consider: When trusting God becomes unpopular, do you go with the crowd or stick with the Lord? Can you believe for the impossible when your situation demands nothing less? What have you seen and experienced that makes it easier to believe for the next crisis?

November 23

NAHSHON

The Messiah Who longs to be with His people

Nahshon the father of Salmon,

Nahshon is of the last generation not allowed to enter the Holy Land. But while they were on the way, Moses oversaw the building of the Tabernacle that became the focal point of Hebrew worship until Solomon built the Temple centuries later.

Numbers 7 outlines the gifts the tribes of Israel brought for the dedication of the new Tabernacle. Each of the tribes brought silver platters, grain offerings, gold containers of incense, burnt offerings and peace offerings of bulls, rams, goats and lambs.

It is at this point that the tribe of Judah starts being listed first instead of fourth. God tells Moses, "Let one leader bring his gift each day for the dedication of the altar" (verse 11). So, on the first day Judah comes with their gift. And the leader of the tribe of Judah who brings the gift is listed as Nahshon, son of Amminadab. This line, which will eventually lead to King David, and then to Jesus Christ, is taking a position of leadership within Judah, and Judah is taking a leadership position among the twelve tribes. And the first occasion where that leadership is recorded is in giving gifts to worship God. If you're going to lead, take the lead in honoring God. It's a great place to start.

The Tabernacle was a place where God's glory appears, where God meets with Moses, and served as the center around which the tribes of Israel camped. But it was intended to be portable and temporary.

In the time of Nahshon, there were two views of the idea of a "dwelling place" for God. On the one hand, Moses prayed in Deuteronomy 26:15, "Now look down from your holy dwelling place in heaven and bless your people ..." Moses sees God's dwelling place as being in heaven even after the Tabernacle was built.

But on the other hand, the Tabernacle was intended to be another dwelling place for God where He could meet with His people on a limited basis. Contemplating the building of the Temple, God said in 2 Samuel 7:6, "I have never lived in a house, from the day I brought the Israelites out of Egypt until this very day. I have always moved from one place to another with a tent and a Tabernacle as my dwelling."

Talking about the Tabernacle, Psalm 84:1 says, "How lovely is your dwelling place, O Lord of Heaven's armies."

But the Tabernacle and Temple weren't close enough to humanity to satisfy God's desire to be with us. "So the Word [that is, Jesus] became human and **made his home among us.** He was full of unfailing love and faithfulness. And we have seen his glory, the glory of the Father's one and only Son" (John 1:14).

In the end, John writes that he "heard a loud shout from the throne, saying, 'Look, God's home is now among his people! He will live with them, and they will be his people. God himself will be with them. He will wipe every tear from their eyes, and there will be no more death or sorrow or crying or pain. All these things are gone forever'" (Revelation 21:3-4). Or as the King James Version puts it, "Behold, the Tabernacle of God is with men."

Nahshon would have loved to see it.

Consider: Do you long for God's presence as much as He longs to be with you?

November 24

SALMON

The Messiah Who declares the old life gone

Salmon the father of Boaz, whose mother was Rahab,

There are only a few women mentioned in this genealogy. It wasn't the common practice of the day to include them in such lists. When Matthew decided to include the name of one of the women, it's there for a reason because it helps to tell the story.

Salmon came of age during the wilderness journeys and was part of the army that Joshua led in the conquest of Canaan.

Before invading, Joshua sent two spies to investigate Jericho. While the text doesn't tell us, I suspect one of these men was Salmon. The spies end up in the home of a prostitute named Rahab, and she tells the spies how the Jericho residents are melting in fear of the invading Israelites. But more than expressing fear, she takes it a step further and says, "The Lord your God is the supreme God of the heavens above and the earth below" (Joshua 2:11).

Unlike the other people of Jericho, she's decided to put her faith in the God of the Israelites. She knows she must choose a side and decides to be on the Lord's side. She hides the spies and helps plan their escape. She asks that her family be spared when the invasion comes.

Joshua honors the deal the spies made, saying, "Keep your promise. Go to the prostitute's house and bring her out, along with all her family" (Joshua 6:22). "So, Joshua spared Rahab the prostitute and her relatives who were with her in the house, because she had hidden the spies Joshua sent to Jericho. And she lives among the

Israelites to this day" (verse 25). "To this day" would be at the time the book of Joshua was written, probably at the end of Joshua's years of conquest.

But more than just "living among the Israelites," she found a home marrying one of the sons of a leading families in Israel, which is why I suspect he was perhaps one of the spies. She was accepted as being one of the people because she had put her trust in God and proved that faith by her deeds.

As the song by the late General John Gowans says,

> *They shall come from the east,*
> *they shall come from the west,*
>
> *And sit down in the Kingdom of God;*
>
> *Both the rich and the poor,*
> *the despised, the distressed,*
>
> *They'll sit down in the Kingdom of God.*
>
> ***And none will ask what they have been,***
> ***provided that their robes are clean;***
>
> *They shall come from the east,*
> *they shall come from the west,*
>
> *And sit down in the Kingdom of God.*

It didn't matter what she was before. Now she was a woman of faith, worthy to be married to Salmon, son of Nahshon, Judah's leader.

And so it was with Christ. He, too, chose prostitutes to inherit the Kingdom. Didn't matter where they came from once they put their faith in Him. "This means that anyone who belongs to Christ has become a new person. The old life is gone; a new life has begun!" (2 Corinthians 5:17).

Consider: Can you accept that God considers your old life extinct, or does guilt from the past keep you from experiencing the Lord's joy? Do you let other believers' pasts go, or do you hold it against them when God does not?

November 25

BOAZ

The Messiah Who redeems people of all nations

Boaz the father of Obed, whose mother was Ruth,

Once again, we get one of those rare generations where Matthew has chosen to include the name of a woman in the genealogy. And again, this is because you'd miss an important part of the story if you left Ruth out.

Many of us have read the book of Ruth and think, "What a great guy this Boaz must have been." But you might look at it in another way when you realize that Boaz's mother was Rahab the former prostitute. No doubt he heard the story of her heroism at the invasion of Jericho, and how his father had accepted and loved her in her newfound faith.

Now Boaz is confronted with another foreign woman of faith in need of rescuing. Ruth had married into a Jewish family in her homeland of Moab. Her husband, her brother-in-law and father-in-law all died, leaving her impoverished with her mother-in-law and sister-in-law remaining.

Mother Naomi decided to go back home to the Promised Land and encouraged her daughters-in-law to stay in Moab and find new husbands there. Ruth refused, saying, "Don't ask me to leave you and turn back. Wherever you go, I will go; wherever you live, I will live. Your people will be my people, and your God will be my God" (Ruth 1:16).

Boaz comes into the story as a "kinsman-redeemer," that is, a relative of Ruth's dead husband, someone who can rescue her from poverty and make her part of the family again. But there's a slight problem, and I'm not talking about the technicality that there was a closer relative available who wasn't interested in doing his family duty.

Deuteronomy 23:3,6 required that "No Ammonite or Moabite or any of their descendants for ten generations may be admitted to the assembly of the Lord… As long as you live, you must never promote the welfare and prosperity of the Ammonites or Moabites." This Law was written to keep the influence of the polytheistic, idol worshipping, child-sacrificing pagans far away from the people of Israel. God said, "Just stay away. Don't bring that stuff into your backyard." Sadly, they pretty much ignored this law in later generations.

But Boaz saw something here beyond the fact that she was from Moab. He realized her faith and character mattered more than her heritage. "I also know about everything you have done for your mother-in-law since the death of your husband. I have heard how you left your father and mother and your own land to live here among complete strangers. May the Lord, the God of Israel, under whose wings you have come to take refuge, reward you fully for what you have done" (Ruth 2:11-12). She had said, "Your God will be my God," and so in Boaz' eyes she wasn't really a Moabite anymore. **Maybe he learned that from Dad.**

Jesus came, not caring about nationalities and heritage. To Him it was always about faith. And that's why He will be honored in Heaven, where they will sing "a new song with these words: 'You are worthy… For you were slaughtered, and your blood has ransomed people for God from **every tribe and language and people and nation**'" (Revelation 5:9). He's our "kinsman-redeemer," rescuing us and making us part of God's family.

Consider: Are you able to accept believers that are different from you as being equal in God's sight? How far are you willing to go to welcome new believers who come from a background foreign to Christianity? What about foreign to your own country and culture?

November 26

OBED

The Messiah Who comes to serve, not be served

Obed the father of Jesse,

Obed comes into the world in the closing chapter of the book of Ruth:

> *So Boaz took Ruth into his home, and she became his wife. When he slept with her, the Lord enabled her to become pregnant, and she gave birth to a son. Then the women of the town said to Naomi, "Praise the Lord, who has now provided a redeemer for your family! May this child be famous in Israel. May he restore your youth and care for you in your old age. For he is the son of your daughter-in-law who loves you and has been better to you than seven sons!"*

> *Naomi took the baby and cuddled him to her breast. And she cared for him as if he were her own. The neighbor women said, "Now at last Naomi has a son again!" And they named him Obed.*

Interestingly, while Obed is Ruth's child, the neighbor women and even Naomi herself treated the child as if he belonged to Grandma. I've watched my wife interact with our three grandsons enough to see where this is coming from. Grandsons are a great blessing, and you love 'em like they're your own.

While Ruth had married the kinsman-redeemer, Naomi was rescued from poverty too. The neighbor women realized that this newborn boy cared for Grandma in her old age. And Naomi wanted to care for him as if he were her own. I'm pretty sure Ruth would have been just fine with it.

Hence, he was named, "Obed," which means, "one who serves." The Jewish commentary called the Targum interprets this to mean, "one who serves God," but in context it sure looks like what they really meant was that he was going to serve and take care of Grandma!

The Messiah came from Obed's line some thirty generations later. In the middle of an argument, Jesus said He's operating on the same principle as Obed:

> *Then they began to argue among themselves about who would be the greatest among them. Jesus told them, "In this world the kings and great men lord it over their people, yet they are called 'friends of the people.' But among you it will be different. Those who are the greatest among you should take the lowest rank, and the leader should be like a servant. Who is more important, the one who sits at the table or the one who serves? The one who sits at the table, of course. But not here! For I am among you as* **one who serves**. (Luke 22:24-27).

He went on to demonstrate His servanthood by washing their feet.

> *After washing their feet, he put on his robe again and sat down and asked, "Do you understand what I was doing? You call me 'Teacher' and 'Lord,' and you are right, because that's what I am. And since I, your Lord and Teacher, have washed your feet, you ought to wash each other's feet. I have given you an example to follow. Do as I have done to you* (John 13:12-15).

In other words, "Be like Obed."

Consider: What are some practical ways you can serve others in a way that makes a difference? What unmet needs are there in your church that you could take care of?

November 27

JESSE

The Messiah Who would be misunderstood and rejected

and Jesse the father of King David.

It's been a busy few years.

The high priesthood of Eli has come crashing down (1 Samuel 4:18), leaving him and his sons dead. God has raised up Samuel as His prophet.

Samuel has anointed Israel's first King, Saul, who has turned out to be a disaster. The people are surprised to find that height and good looks aren't the best things to look for when picking a king. Even the king's son, Jonathan, knows the dynasty of Saul isn't going to last. In America we call this a "one term" president who is considered a "lame duck" the day after mid-terms.

Wars with surrounding nations, especially Philistia, are almost an annual affair, continuing the pattern from the period of the Judges. God calls Samuel to anoint the next king, even though he won't take the throne for some time. Uneasy, Samuel goes to the house of Jesse, still an important family in Judah, to find one of his sons to anoint. God warns Samuel in 1 Samuel 16:7 not to make his selection based on appearance or height, especially since that didn't turn out so well in choosing Saul.

Jesse has eight sons, and somebody had to stay out in the field watching the sheep. Jesse brings in his seven oldest sons and has the youngest stay with the sheep. It's not a strange decision. It seems to make sense that the chosen one would be among the seven older sons. It just didn't occur to Jesse that David could be the choice. But as God tells Samuel, "People judge by outward appearance, but the Lord looks at the heart." Did

Jesse realize God's criteria? Unlikely. Did he know his son David's heart was fixed on God? Maybe. Did he know David's love for God poured out in faith that defeated lions and bears, as well as in music and poetry? Maybe. But even if he knew these things, it still didn't cross his mind that David could possibly be God's choice to be king.

Jesus faced similar issues.

> *He returned to Nazareth, his hometown. When he taught there in the synagogue, everyone was amazed and said, "Where does he get this wisdom and the power to do miracles?" Then they scoffed, "He's just the carpenter's son, and we know Mary, his mother, and his brothers—James, Joseph, Simon, and Judas. All his sisters live right here among us. Where did he learn all these things?" And they were deeply offended and refused to believe in him.*
>
> *Then Jesus told them, "A prophet is honored everywhere except in his own hometown and among his own family"* (Matthew 13:54-57).

They misjudged Jesus, thinking they knew Him. They figured He was a nobody and made the same mistake Jesse did: "This can't possibly be the guy."

Good thing Jesus doesn't look at us that way. He looks at us and sees what could be. Others saw former tax collectors, prostitutes, and so on. Jesus saw powerful evangelists who turned the world upside down. He tears up the playbook that expects the sinner to come to the church and instead insists that the church go to seek and save the lost in His name.

As depicted in the streaming drama, *The Chosen*, Jesus says, "Get used to different."

Consider: Do you leave room in your prayers for God to act in unexpected ways? Or do you have Him so well figured out that He can never act "out of the box"? If God is sovereign, you can't pin Him down.

November 28

DAVID

The Messiah of the heart, not just the head

David was the father of Solomon, whose mother had been Uriah's wife,

David is credited with writing much of the Psalms, and his musical talent is noted long before he became king. In fact, some of his best stuff comes from the period when he was being chased by Saul trying to end his life.

I've found in my life that when the family has a crisis, that's often when the music writing starts to flow. There's something about being backed into a corner and being forced to rely on God that brings out the composition juices.

Psalms is a very different book than Genesis—Job. Up to this point, the books of the Bible have been primarily about conveying facts of history. But the focus of Psalms is about conveying the feelings of the writers. We've gone from stories to emotions; from head stuff to heart stuff.

God understands the importance of both facts and emotions. He didn't design us as emotionless Vulcans[1]. And often, heart-speaking is what draws people to Him more effectively than head knowledge.

David speaks this language. And again and again, caught up in the ebb-and-flow of writing musical lyrics, engaging the heart and feelings, the Holy Spirit speaks prophetically through him.

---

1 In the television and movies franchises of *Star Trek*, Vulcans are an alien race that are guided solely by logic, denying the need for emotion.

This remarkable man of God sung prophetically of the coming Messiah throughout his lifetime. It's fitting that he should be the generation that capped off Matthew's first group of fourteen.

This is one of those times a woman is mentioned, and the story of David isn't complete without mentioning his fall from grace with Bathsheba. Regarding this incident, David begged the Lord, "Do not banish me from your presence, and don't take your Holy Spirit from me" (Psalm 51:11).

David had sinned, committing adultery and murder, but God's Spirit hadn't left him. He still had enough of a connection to God to realize he was in danger of ending up as his predecessor had: "Now the Spirit of the Lord had left Saul" (1 Samuel 16:14).

Saul had sinned, and when confronted, he made excuses. David sinned, and when confronted, he repented. That's what made him "a man after God's own heart" (1 Samuel 13:14).

For generations after, David was viewed as the model king. And Jesus was known as the "Son of David," even though many generations came between the two. Like David, Jesus longed to please His Father. But unlike David, He didn't sin (Hebrews 4:15).

Consider: Are you a woman or man after God's own heart? How you respond when confronted about sin says a lot. The one after God's heart returns and repents; others try to justify themselves and avoid dealing with what they did.

November 29

SOLOMON

The Messiah Who delights in giving good things

Solomon the father of Rehoboam,

Solomon was not even close to being David's eldest son, but his father, urged on by his mother, saw him as the worthiest candidate.

At this point the genealogies in Matthew and Luke diverge. Luke starts tracing the lineage of Christ through Solomon's half-brother, Nathan. While Luke's genealogy is not explicit, most interpreters believe that he is tracing the line through to Mary while Matthew goes through to Joseph.

There's an important point here which we'll look at when we get to December 12, Jehoiachin and his brothers. Both Matthew's and Luke's genealogies are necessary to establish Jesus' right to the throne of David.

Solomon is known as the compiler of Proverbs and author of many of them, as well as the writer of Ecclesiastes and Solomon's Song of Songs. "He composed some 3,000 proverbs and wrote 1,005 songs" (1 Kings 4:32). There are a lot of interpreters who think the Song of Songs is an allegory for the relationship between Christ and His bride, the Church, but personally I think the book is a bit too sexualized for that interpretation.

Early in his reign, Solomon went to Gibeah and sacrificed 1,000 burnt offerings. Clearly his credit limit was a lot higher than mine. "That night the Lord appeared to Solomon in a dream, and God said, 'What do you want? Ask, and I will give it to you!'" (1 Kings 3:5).

"What do you want?" Jesus had a habit of asking that very same question.

He asks it of two blind men in Jericho in Matthew 20:32. He asks it of Bartimaeus, another blind man, in Mark 10:51. There's another Jericho blind man, alone this time, in Luke 18:41. When two of John's disciples came to see Jesus, He asked the same question to them in John 1:38. There are probably a number of other times Jesus asked this that aren't recorded.

Not every time Jesus asked this question did people get what they wanted. The mother of James and John, seeking positions for her sons, was also asked the question. I'm pretty sure they didn't like the answer to their request much.

When someone comes to Jesus, **He does have an agenda.** God wants to conform us to the image of His Son (Romans 8:29). He wants us the be His witnesses (Acts 1:8). He wants us to mature in Him (Ephesians 4:13). He wants us to thrive on Him as the True Vine (John 15:4) and grow the fruit of His Spirit (Galatians 5:22-23).

But Jesus isn't only interested in *His* agenda. What's important to us matters to Him. He wants to know what *we* want, and He delights in giving us good things (Luke 11:11-13). When He asks, give a good answer. Solomon did, and God was pleased with his request for wisdom to rule his Kingdom. He threw in wealth and safety from his enemies as bonuses. The great heart of our Savior loves to say, "Yes, of course!" as often as He can, within the scope of His Father's purposes.

Consider: If the Lord appeared to you today and asked, "What do you want?", what would you say? How would you respond if He said, "Let me tell you what *I* want."?

November 30

REHOBOAM

The Messiah Who disciplines

Rehoboam the father of Abijah,

In Solomon's old age, his heart was turned away from God because of all the foreign women he had married. He built idols and shrines contrary to God's commandments.

His son, Rehoboam, took over the throne at age 41. But he acted like a spoiled teenager. He fired all the experienced advisors and took advice from younger, inexperienced men who told him that the middle of an economic meltdown was a great time to raise taxes. Funny how this mistake gets made over and over through history, always with tragic results. So, God ripped away most of Solomon's kingdom, giving it to Jeroboam, one of Solomon's officials. Ten tribes out of twelve were gone.

God was trying to get Rehoboam's attention. He doubled down on his father's idolatry. It seemed Rehoboam and Jeroboam (in the Northern Kingdom) were competing, trying to outdo each other in rebellion against God.

God sent multiple prophets to the Northern Kingdom, to no avail. None came to visit Rehoboam. As the heart of the nation decayed, religious prostitution took root in Judah. David committed adultery with one woman. Solomon's felt the need to have 1,000 women, but at least maintained a semblance of legitimacy through marriage and concubinage. But the next generation turned to both male and female prostitution in some twisted mockery of worship. Once sex gets out of its God-ordained boundaries, it destroys everything in its path.

"In the fifth year of King Rehoboam's reign, King Shishak of Egypt came up and attacked Jerusalem. He ransacked the treasuries of the Lord's Temple and the royal palace; he stole everything, including all the gold shields Solomon had made" (1 Kings 14:25-26). I can hear the Lord saying, "Do I have your attention yet?"

In John 15:2, Jesus talks about how He prunes the branches on His vine because He desperately wants fruitfulness. And the writer to the Hebrews follows up on this:

> *And have you forgotten the encouraging words God spoke to you as his children? He said, "My child, don't make light of the Lord's discipline, and don't give up when he corrects you. For the Lord disciplines those he loves, and he punishes each one he accepts as his child."* Hebrews 12:5-6

Rehoboam was experiencing firsthand the painful process God uses in pruning. I believe today God is pruning His church. In the United States over the past decades, multiple denominations, most recently the Southern Baptist Convention, have suffered through sexual scandal. The Roman Catholic Church is still dealing with the fallout 25 years later. A number of senior pastors of megachurches have fallen from grace as well.

God will simply not put up with sexual sin in His church. He will not put up with abusing children. He will not put up with leaders who merely transfer the offenders to avoid scandal and allow them to abuse again. No denomination or local church is immune, including ours. Pruning is painful. Jesus quoted Psalm 69:9 when He turned over the tables of those who had turned the Temple into an abusive marketplace. "Passion for your house has consumed me."

Rehoboam stands as a warning. The Messiah to come, loving and gentle as He is, will pick up a whip when He needs to.

Consider: How would you respond if Jesus started turning over the tables of habitual compromise in your life? What would you say to a fellow believer going under the Lord's rod of discipline?

December 1

ABIJAH

The Messiah Who isn't fooled by fakery

Abijah the father of Asa,

Abijah, who only ruled for three years, was a man of contradictions. On the one hand, 2 Chronicles 13 records him bravely and loudly proclaiming the supremacy of the Lord over his idolatrous rivals. He took on King Jeroboam, still ruler in the north, outnumbered two to one. He challenged, "Listen to me! Don't you realize that the Lord, the God of Israel, made a lasting covenant with David, giving him and his descendants the throne of Israel forever? Yet Jeroboam son of Nebat, a mere servant of David's son Solomon, rebelled against his master." This is the political argument.

He went on to talk the religious angle: "But you have chased away the priests of the Lord (the descendants of Aaron) and the Levites, and you have appointed your own priests, just like the pagan nations. You let anyone become a priest these days! …But as for us, the Lord is our God, and we have not abandoned him…We are following the instructions of the Lord our God, but you have abandoned him. So you see, God is with us. He is our leader."

Great, stirring speech until you realize he didn't really mean a word of it. It was all a publicity stunt to rally his own troops and intimidate the enemy. First Kings 15 gives the rest of the story. "He committed the same sins as his father before him, and he was not faithful to the Lord his God, as his ancestor David had been."

When Christ came, "No one needed to tell him about human nature, for he knew what was in each person's heart" (John 2:25). In Matthew 23, Jesus called out the Pharisees of His day for the same kind of fake show-faith.

- "They don't practice what they teach." (v.4)
- "Everything they do is for show." (v.5)
- "Hypocrites! For you are so careful to clean the outside of the cup and the dish, but inside you are filthy—full of greed and self-indulgence!" (v.25)
- "Hypocrites! For you are like whitewashed tombs—beautiful on the outside but filled on the inside with dead people's bones and all sorts of impurity. Outwardly you look like righteous people, but inwardly your hearts are filled with hypocrisy and lawlessness." (vv. 27-28)

Jesus wanted genuine followers, not just people who only claimed to belong to Him. He warned,

Not everyone who calls out to me, 'Lord! Lord!' will enter the Kingdom of Heaven. Only those who actually do the will of my Father in heaven will enter. On judgment day many will say to me, 'Lord! Lord! We prophesied in your name and cast out demons in your name and performed many miracles in your name.' But I will reply, 'I never knew you. Get away from me, you who break God's laws.' Matthew 7:21-23

Jesus' brother, James, later added: "But don't just listen to God's word. You must do what it says. Otherwise, you are only fooling yourselves" (James 1:22).

Advent isn't a show. Christmas isn't a pageant with cute kids at church. It's about *really* being His follower, not just looking like it.

Consider: Are you putting into practice what you've learned from God's Word? Or are you merely keeping up appearances? You can fool everybody except the One that really matters.

December 2

ASA

The Messiah Who brings peace despite outward trouble

Asa the father of Jehoshaphat,

Asa was a welcome change from his predecessors; he "did what was pleasing and good in the sight of the Lord his God" (2 Chronicles 14:2). Asa was king for 41 years. This would be like Ronald Reagan still being president in 2022. Over the course of his reign in Judah, Israel in the north had Nadab, Baasha, Elah, Zimri, Tibni, Omri come and go, and Ahab started his reign of terror. God started to send prophets to confront the rampant, festering sin, though these early prophets didn't write books.

This is another case where you need to look at both Kings and Chronicles to get the whole story. First Kings 15:16 reports that "There was constant war between King Asa of Judah and King Baasha of Israel." Baasha accounted for 24 of Asa's 41 years on the throne. There were border issues regarding a town called Ramah.

But 2 Chronicles 14:5-6 indicates that "Asa's kingdom enjoyed a period of peace. During those peaceful years, he was able to build up the fortified towns throughout Judah. No one tried to make war against him at this time, for the Lord was giving him rest from his enemies." That chapter also mentions a little invasion by Ethiopia – only 1,000,000 men involved – which the Lord struck down after Asa's fervent prayer.

There was also palace intrigue as Asa deposed his grandmother Maacah from her position as queen mother, because of her idol worship. He "removed all the detestable idols from the land of Judah and Benjamin and in the towns he had captured in the hill country of Ephraim. And he repaired the altar of the Lord, which stood in front of the entry room of the Lord's Temple" (2 Chronicles 15:8).

Word spread about the king who wanted to faithfully serve God, and some of the people from Ephraim, Manasseh and Simeon moved out of the northern kingdom and started living in Judah. "For many from Israel had moved to Judah during Asa's reign when they saw that the Lord his God was with him" (2 Chronicles 15:9). "They sought God eagerly, and he was found by them. So the Lord gave them rest on every side" (2 Chronicles 15:15 NIV).

How can constant war, an invasion, border disputes and internal strife equal "rest on every side?" Because Asa and his people found that God can give you rest even when the world around you is falling apart.

Jesus was known as the "Prince of Peace" (Isaiah 9:6) despite His life being surrounded by controversy and conflict. He said, "Come to me, all of you who are weary and carry heavy burdens, and I will give you rest. Take my yoke upon you. Let me teach you, because I am humble and gentle at heart, and you will find rest for your souls" (Matthew 11:28-9). Hebrews 4:6-7 tells us that "God's rest is there for people to enter, but those who first heard this good news failed to enter because they disobeyed God. So God set another time for entering his rest, and that time is today."

Jesus came so that "you will experience God's peace, which exceeds anything we can understand. His peace will guard your hearts and minds as you live in Christ Jesus" (Philippians 4:7).

Come, Prince of Peace. We need You.

Consider: When troubles come, do you still have that deep sense that everything is going to be alright, that God is in control? Or does your peace leave when the good times end? You can't think your way into inward peace; it comes through living in Him.

December 3

JEHOSHAPHAT

The Messiah Who handles what we can't

Jehoshaphat the father of Jehoram,

Unlike the old expression, "Jumping Jehoshaphat," there is no record in the Scripture of Jehoshaphat ever jumping. There are, however, several references to him *standing*. Standing to pray. Standing to rally his people to depend on God. Standing up in King Ahab's court to check what the Lord's will is and not just relying on pagan prophets. Standing against the tide of foreign gods always trying to reestablish a foothold in his kingdom.

He saw the throne of Israel turn over from Ahab to Ahaziah to Joram. He heard about Elijah's many confrontations with Ahab and Elisha's often miraculous ministry at the time of Ahaziah.

Twice Jehoshaphat made the mistake of allying his kingdom with the north. God used this first alliance to bring Ahab to an end in battle, though the prophet Jehu told Jehoshaphat he shouldn't have been there in the first place. Later he allied again with the north to build a fleet of ships, all wrecked before sailing.

But despite these errors, Jehoshaphat generally trusted God and served Him well. This is because he again and again demonstrated his dependence on God. He appointed godly judges and Scripture teachers to spread throughout his land.

When his enemies the Moabites, Ammonites and Meunites united to attack him, he gathered his people together:

> He prayed, "O Lord, God of our ancestors, you alone are the God who is in heaven. You are ruler of all the kingdoms of the earth. You are powerful and

mighty; no one can stand against you... We are powerless against this mighty army that is about to attack us. We do not know what to do, but we are looking to you for help" (2 Chronicles 20:6,12).

God raised up a prophet to tell them: "You will not have to fight this battle... stand firm and see the deliverance the Lord will give you" (2 Chronicles 20:17 NIV). They praised the Lord, and the enemy alliance was destroyed. Did you notice that word, "stand," again?

Jehoshaphat understood that **everything depended on his dependence.** The coming Messiah taught: "Apart from me you can do nothing" (John 15:5).

And the dependence that Jesus called for in us, He modelled:

- "I tell you the truth, the Son can do nothing by himself. He does only what he sees the Father doing. Whatever the Father does, the Son also does" (John 5:19).

- "I can do nothing on my own. I judge as God tells me. Therefore, my judgment is just, because I carry out the will of the one who sent me, not my own will" (John 5:30).

- "I do nothing on my own but say only what the Father taught me" (John 8:28).

In Christ we can know that "after the battle you will still be standing firm" (Ephesians 6:13). Or jump, if you really feel like it.

Consider: Try to take measure of your reliance on God versus relying on your own capabilities. Do you depend on Him even when what you're facing will be easy to handle on your own? Do you live the verse, "Apart from me you can do nothing?"

December 4

JEHORAM

The Messiah Who restores what has fallen

Jehoram the father of Uzziah,

This is one of those times where Matthew chooses to leave out some details. Jehoram had a rather short reign, only seven years, and it didn't end well. He died of an intestinal disease which led to his bowels coming out. Definitely not on my list of favorite ways to leave this world.

"Jehoram followed the example of the kings of Israel and was as wicked as King Ahab, for he had married one of Ahab's daughters" (2 Chronicles 21:6). This was the same Ahab who had the confrontation with Elijah on Mount Carmel. The marriage probably happened in the context of Jehoshaphat's ill-conceived brief alliance with the north. Queen Athaliah's influence on her husband was stronger than good king dad, and Jehoram took the kingdom back into idol worship. Elijah the prophet tried to warn him, but he didn't listen. In the end, "No one was sorry when he died" (2 Chronicles 21:20)

Once he was dead, Athaliah proclaimed herself queen and so the daughter of Israel's king actually ruled Judah. She executed a campaign to wipe out the entire royal family to ensure she could not be challenged.

It didn't work. Her grandson, Jehoash, was hidden in the Temple for seven years, after which the high priest anointed the boy in a *coup d'etat* that left the queen dead. Jehoash, also known as Joash, having been raised in the Temple, served God faithfully and suppressed Ba'al worship in his kingdom…until his mentor, the high priest, died. Then it was back to Ba'al again.

He was succeeded by his son, Amaziah, after being assassinated. Amaziah ruled for 29 years, but 25 of them were in co-regency with his son, Uzziah. So, he wasn't really in charge for long.

This whole period was a mess of tumult and uprising. Jehu, Jehoahaz and Jehoash came and went in the north during this period. Particularly confusing was the period when both kingdoms had a Jehoash on the throne.

Matthew chose to leave that whole disaster out of his genealogy. In his view, Uzziah was the next really real, legitimate king. The line descended from Ahab and Jezebel was blotted out until the fourth generation. This fulfills the command in Exodus 20:5:

> *You must not bow down to [idols] or worship them, for I, the Lord your God, am a jealous God who will not tolerate your affection for any other gods. I lay the sins of the parents upon their children; the entire family is affected— even children in the third and fourth generations of those who reject me.*

It was during this time that Jonah made his trip to Nineveh. If he had had a GPS, it would have said, "Recalculating."

Prophets predicting doom. Assassinations. Ba'al and Ashtoreth worship in God's Temple. Is it any wonder people wanted to put all this behind them? And in that context, once Uzziah finally came to the throne, Amos looked forward and prophesied: "In that day I will restore the fallen house of David. I will repair its damaged walls. From the ruins I will rebuild it and restore its former glory" (Amos 9:11).

There were still some good kings to come; but not until the coming of Christ would the fallen house of David truly be restored.

Consider: What areas of your life are broken or fallen? What would you have Christ rebuild, knowing it may take a new form in the restoration process? What would it take to trust Him with the repairs?

December 5

UZZIAH

The Messiah Who brings down the proud

Uzziah the father of Jotham,

Uzziah is most famous for dying, memorialized in Isaiah's prophecy marking "the year that King Uzziah died" (Isaiah 6:1). How he died was rather grotesque, like some of his predecessors who had similarly bad ends.

Uzziah was crowned at age 16 and ruled for 52 years. In 2023 that could be compared to him beginning his reign right after the Apollo 11 moon landing. "Uzziah sought God during the days of Zechariah, who taught him to fear God. And as long as the king sought guidance from the Lord, God gave him success" (2 Chronicles 26:5). This Zechariah was probably the high priest, not the prophet who wrote after the Babylonian exile.

He was successful in battles with Philistia, Arabia and Amon. He earned the respect of Egypt. He rebuilt towns and built forts in his territory. He improved the defensive walls around Jerusalem. He had massive herds and flocks, and he "was also a man who loved the soil. He had many workers who cared for his farms and vineyards, both on the hillsides and in the fertile valleys" (2 Chronicles 26:10). "His fame spread far and wide, for the Lord gave him marvelous help, and he became very powerful" (2 Chronicles 26:15).

But "when he had become powerful, he also became proud, which led to his downfall" (verse 16).

Perhaps you know of a recent American president who was tremendously successful in foreign policy, had his enemies on the run, and had a booming economy, but also had an ego the size of Montana. I wonder what Uzziah would have done with a Twitter account. His pride led him to think himself worthy of the priestly duty of offering incense in the Temple. His arrogance led to a judgment of leprosy, so the guy who loved the adulation of the crowds spent his last years in isolation.

Jesus' mother, Mary, singing prophetically in the *Magnificat* (Luke 1:55) said, "He has brought down princes from their thrones and exalted the humble."

Jesus on multiple occasions, said, "Those who exalt themselves will be humbled, and those who humble themselves will be exalted" (e.g., Matthew 23:12).

And in the Sermon on the Mount, He told the crowd, "God blesses those who are humble, for they will inherit the whole earth" (Matthew 5:5).

Later He said, "So anyone who becomes as humble as this little child is the greatest in the Kingdom of Heaven" (Matthew 18:4).

He told a story about choosing seats at a banquet in such a way to avoid coming off as proud and ending up shamed; one should take the humblest seat in the room. (Luke 14:7-11)

Herod the Great, who tried to kill Jesus along with the other boys of Bethlehem, died by being consumed by worms. As an adult, Jesus embarrassed the Pharisees every time they thought they had Him in a "gotcha" moment. He confounded the kings of His day and left Pilate wondering what truth was. Pilate, too, ended a broken man.

Christ the humbler of the proud was also the lifter of the brokenhearted.

Consider: Look for places of pride in your life. Jesus would rather take down your pride than take you down altogether; but He won't leave pride unchecked.

December 6

JOTHAM

The Messiah of one more chance

Jotham the father of Ahaz,

"King Jotham became powerful because he was careful to live in obedience to the Lord his God" (2 Chronicles 27:6). He started off in a coregency with his father when Uzziah could no longer fulfill the duties of his office due to leprosy. But Uzziah's influence—and that of his mother, a high priest's daughter—clearly helped Jotham make good decisions and stay faithful to the Lord.

Meanwhile, the northern kingdom was circling the drain. Pekah was the penultimate king in the north and soon the Assyrians brought Israel to an end.

It was in this environment—godly leadership on one side of the border, and horrors on the other – that the prophet Isaiah shared God's Word. His influence was primarily to the northern kingdom, but his five-decade ministry and extensive writings had to have reached Jotham.

Isaiah added more to the prophetic literature about the coming Messiah than anyone since King David, and his writings included many specific predictions about Jesus. It should also be noted that Isaiah often writes with no distinction between Christ's first coming and His return at the end of days. From Isaiah's point of view, both are "in the last days."

You'll recall from yesterday's review of Uzziah that he was a "man of the soil" and had many vineyards. So, his son would have understood Isaiah's story of the vineyard:

> *My beloved had a vineyard on a rich and fertile hill. He plowed the land, cleared its stones, and planted it with the best vines. Then he waited for a harvest of sweet grapes, but the grapes that grew were bitter.*
>
> *What more could I have done for my vineyard that I have not already done?*
>
> *Now let me tell you what I will do to my vineyard: I will tear down its hedges and let it be destroyed* (Isaiah 5:1-6).

Jesus told a number of stories about vineyards, because they were such an important part of the culture and people understood what He was talking about. But Isaiah's story finds its best parallel when Jesus was talking about a fig tree:

> *A man planted a fig tree in his garden and came again and again to see if there was any fruit on it, but he was always disappointed. Finally, he said to his gardener, 'I've waited three years, and there hasn't been a single fig! Cut it down. It's just taking up space in the garden.'*
>
> *The gardener answered, 'Sir, give it one more chance. Leave it another year, and I'll give it special attention and plenty of fertilizer. If we get figs next year, fine. If not, then you can cut it down'* (Luke 13:6-9).

Our Savior is not in a hurry to bring judgement. He wants to do everything He can to win us over, give us every chance. "The Lord isn't really being slow about his promise [to bring judgement], as some people think. No, he is being patient for your sake. He does not want anyone to be destroyed, but wants everyone to repent" (2 Peter 3:9).

Jesus will be able to look His Father in the eye at the last day and say, "What more could I have done?" He's the Messiah of "one more chance."

He calls all to salvation. He gives them every opportunity to repent and believe. But eventually, judgment will come, as the northern kingdom will soon find out.

Consider: How willing are you to give another chance to those who have wronged you? Have you given up and written someone off before reaching "seventy times seven?"

December 7
AHAZ

The Virgin-born Messiah

Ahaz the father of Hezekiah,

As we move on to Ahaz, Isaiah is still prophesying, and Pekah is still king in Israel. Ahaz faced invasion from not only his northern neighbor Israel, but Syria as well. Isaiah assured Ahaz the invasion wouldn't take place. Through the prophet, God told Ahaz, "Unless your faith is firm, I cannot make you stand firm" (Isaiah 7:9).

Later, Isaiah tried to continue to encourage faith in Ahaz by telling him, "Ask the Lord your God for a sign of confirmation, Ahaz. Make it as difficult as you want—as high as heaven or as deep as the place of the dead" (Isaiah 7:11).

Ahaz responds by citing Deuteronomy 6:16, "You must not test the Lord your God." But Ahaz takes the verse out of context. Besides, he's a Ba'al worshipper. The passage warns against testing God "as you did when you complained at Massah," a time when Israel was showing a lack of faith and rebellion against the Lord. Other times in Scripture, asking God for a test was rewarded, such as when Gideon put out his fleece (see Judges 6:17).

Faithless tests that try God's patience are forbidden. But when someone is trying to have faith, and asks God for help, it's okay.

That is why Jesus didn't give signs when the Pharisees demanded proof that He was the Messiah. The request didn't come from a place of faith. (Matthew 16:4)

So, Isaiah says, "You won't ask God for a sign when he offers? Then He'll give you one." (My paraphrase.) I think there were two. First, he says, "Look! The virgin will conceive a child! She will give birth to a son and will call him Immanuel (which means 'God is with us')," (Isaiah 7:14) which is quoted in the gospels as pointing to the Virgin Birth of Christ.

But there's a second part where he says, "By the time this child is old enough to choose what is right and reject what is wrong, he will be eating yogurt and honey. For before the child is that old, the lands of the two kings you fear so much will both be deserted" (Isaiah 7:15-16). This confuses some people, because the first sentence refers to the coming of Christ over 700 years away at this point, while the second sentence refers to the fall of Syria and Israel coming as soon as "this child" reaches a certain age. What people miss is that Isaiah brought his son, Shear-jashub, along when he saw King Ahaz. So "this child" probably refers to Isaiah's kid, not Jesus.

Isaiah goes on regarding the coming Messiah:

> *For a child is born to us, a son is given to us. The government will rest on his shoulders. And he will be called: Wonderful Counselor, Mighty God, Everlasting Father, Prince of Peace. His government and its peace will never end.* (Isaiah 9:6).

It's particularly apropos that Isaiah made multiple references to the Messiah as a child and bring his own child to the king as an object lesson. You see, Ahaz himself participated in child sacrifice to Ba'al (2 Chronicles 28:2-3). So as Ahaz is leading his country to ruin through sacrificing his own sons, Isaiah predicted that God sent His own Son to be a Savior. Ba'al would not be able to interrupt one of the lines that led to Christ.

Consider: Ponder the titles given to Christ in Isaiah 9:6. How is He *your* Wonderful Counselor? How does He display His mighty power in your life? How is He a Father to you? How does He bring peace into your life?

December 8

HEZEKIAH

The Messiah Who hears and answers prayer

Hezekiah the father of Manasseh,

Hezekiah was king when the northern kingdom of Israel finally fell. King Hoshea and his people were deported to Assyria, leaving few survivors in the land. Assyria later imported substitute people into the land, resulting in the half-Jewish Samaritans.

It was not long before Assyria threatened Judah as well. Unlike his predecessors, "Hezekiah trusted in the Lord, the God of Israel. There was no one like him among all the kings of Judah, either before or after his time. He remained faithful to the Lord in everything, and he carefully obeyed all the commands the Lord had given Moses. So the Lord was with him, and Hezekiah was successful in everything he did. He revolted against the king of Assyria and refused to pay him tribute" (2 Kings 18:5-7).

Sennacherib, king of the Assyrians, came to attack. His messengers taunted the people of Jerusalem by saying God didn't save Israel, and He can't save Judah, either.

Isaiah tried to reassure the king, but Sennacherib turned up the heat with more taunts about other nations Assyria had destroyed and the gods who didn't protect them. This only pushed Hezekiah back to prayer.

> *Now, O Lord our God, rescue us from his power; then all the kingdoms of the earth will know that you alone, O Lord, are God"* (2 Kings 19:19).

Isaiah sent another message to Hezekiah to reassure him, and soon the Assyrian army of 185,000 soldiers was destroyed in one night. Hezekiah's wholehearted trust in God was rewarded, and his people were saved.

Later, Hezekiah became terribly sick and turned to God in prayer once again. And once again Isaiah comforted him, and God healed him. This is another one of those times a faithful believer asked God for a sign and was rewarded, not punished.

It was around this time that Isaiah predicted, "When oppression and destruction have ended and enemy raiders have disappeared, then God will establish one of David's descendants as king. He will rule with mercy and truth. He will always do what is just and be eager to do what is right" (Isaiah 16:4-5). So, if you like Hezekiah, you're *really* going to like Jesus.

> *Out of the stump of David's family will grow a shoot— yes, a new Branch bearing fruit from the old root. And the Spirit of the Lord will rest on him— the Spirit of wisdom and understanding, the Spirit of counsel and might, the Spirit of knowledge and the fear of the Lord* (Isaiah 35:4).

Isaiah predicted Jesus' ministry, death and resurrection in incredible detail. Micah, who had ministered during Jotham and Ahaz, wraps up his ministry under Hezekiah and predicts that the Messiah would be born in Bethlehem.

Hezekiah's faithfulness to the Lord, and his constancy in turning to God when faced with crises, was richly rewarded not only with answers to his prayers, but with the clearest prophecies of the coming of Christ heard by any king. He lived and died with the hope of the One to come, who would bring hope and healing to the people, die for our sins and rise again from the dead. Hezekiah closed his eyes for the final time knowing that he would awaken one day in the eternal kingdom of David's true heir.

Consider: What's your first instinct when crisis looms? Do you try to figure it out, or go straight to prayer? Seeking God in prayer should be your first resort, not your last.

December 9

MANASSEH

The Messiah Who uses pain to draw us to Himself

Manasseh the father of Amon,

Manasseh grew up seeing, or at least hearing about, his faithful father receiving blessings and miraculous answers to prayer. But there are no guarantees that faithful parents will have faithful children, try as they might. A parent can do all the right things and still have their child make bad choices.

In the case of Manasseh, the choices couldn't have been much worse.

> *He rebuilt the pagan shrines his father, Hezekiah, had destroyed. He constructed altars for Baal and set up an Asherah pole, just as King Ahab of Israel had done. He also bowed before all the powers of the heavens and worshiped them... He built these altars for all the powers of the heavens in both courtyards of the Lord's Temple. Manasseh also sacrificed his own son in the fire. He practiced sorcery and divination, and he consulted with mediums and psychics... Manasseh also murdered many innocent people until Jerusalem was filled from one end to the other with innocent blood. This was in addition to the sin that he caused the people of Judah to commit, leading them to do evil in the Lord's sight* (2 Kings 21:3-16).

The Lord sent prophets to confront him. He didn't listen. So, God turned the pain meter up to 11.

The Lord spoke to Manasseh and his people, but they ignored all his warnings. So the Lord sent the commanders of the Assyrian armies, and they took Manasseh prisoner. They put a ring through his nose, bound him in bronze chains, and led him away to Babylon. But while in deep distress, Manasseh sought the Lord his God and sincerely humbled himself before the God of his ancestors. And when he prayed, the Lord listened to him and was moved by his request. So the Lord brought Manasseh back to Jerusalem and to his kingdom. Then Manasseh finally realized that the Lord alone is God!

Manasseh also removed the foreign gods and the idol from the Lord's Temple. He tore down all the altars he had built on the hill where the Temple stood and all the altars that were in Jerusalem, and he dumped them outside the city. Then he restored the altar of the Lord and sacrificed peace offerings and thanksgiving offerings on it. He also encouraged the people of Judah to worship the Lord, the God of Israel (2 Chronicles 33:10-16).

Jesus came preaching a gospel of repentance.

But what do you think about this? A man with two sons told the older boy, 'Son, go out and work in the vineyard today.' The son answered, 'No, I won't go,' but later he changed his mind and went anyway. Then the father told the other son, 'You go,' and he said, 'Yes, sir, I will.' But he didn't go (Matthew 21:28-30).

Manasseh changed his mind and served God. Jesus also told the stories of the lost sheep, the lost coin, and the lost son to illustrate that "there is joy in the presence of God's angels when even one sinner repents" (Luke 15:10).

Consider: How has God used difficult circumstances to redirect you to Himself?

December 10

AMON

The Messiah of the right now

> *Amon the father of Josiah,*

Amon gets five verses in 2 Kings:

> *Amon was twenty-two years old when he became king, and he reigned in Jerusalem two years. His mother was Meshullemeth, the daughter of Haruz from Jotbah. He did what was evil in the Lord's sight, just as his father, Manasseh, had done. He followed the example of his father, worshiping the same idols his father had worshiped. He abandoned the Lord, the God of his ancestors, and he refused to follow the Lord's ways. Then Amon's own officials conspired against him and assassinated him in his palace* (2 Kings 21:19-23).

Chronicles adds no information to his sordid tale.

He probably knew his father's story—how Manasseh had done those very same evil things but had turned his life around by repenting. Perhaps Amon thought he had more time. Maybe he didn't believe his father's warnings about the consequences of breaking God's commandments.

It was under his father's rule that Isaiah prophesied, "This is what the Lord says: 'At just the right time, I will respond to you. On the day of salvation, I will help you'" (Isaiah 49:8). Later, Paul quoted this verse in his letter to the Corinthians, adding, "Indeed, the 'right time' is now. Today is the day of salvation" (2 Corinthians 6:2).

You can't wait until tomorrow to seek the Savior. There might not be a tomorrow for you. Jesus told this story as a warning:

"A rich man had a fertile farm that produced fine crops. He said to himself, 'What should I do? I don't have room for all my crops.' Then he said, 'I know! I'll tear down my barns and build bigger ones. Then I'll have room enough to store all my wheat and other goods. And I'll sit back and say to myself, "My friend, you have enough stored away for years to come. Now take it easy! Eat, drink, and be merry!"'

"But God said to him, 'You fool! You will die this very night. Then who will get everything you worked for?'

"Yes, a person is a fool to store up earthly wealth but not have a rich relationship with God" (Luke 12:16-21).

For in just a little while, the Coming One will come and not delay. And my righteous ones will live by faith. But I will take no pleasure in anyone who turns away. But we are not like those who turn away from God to their own destruction. We are the faithful ones, whose souls will be saved (Hebrews 10:37-39).

Amon missed his chance. He didn't learn from his father's repentance. Christ is coming again. Are you ready for Him?

Consider: Have you accepted Christ as your savior? Knowing *about* Him isn't the same as knowing Him.

December 11

JOSIAH

The Merciful Messiah

> *Josiah was the father of Jehoiachin and his brothers (born at the time of the exile to Babylon).*

In Matthew's genealogy, Josiah is the end of the second group of fourteen. The first ended with David, the second with Josiah, both examples of good kings who loved the Lord.

Josiah assumed the throne at the age of eight due to his father's assassination. "He did what was pleasing in the Lord's sight and followed the example of his ancestor David. He did not turn away from doing what was right" (2 Kings 22:2).

In his eighteenth year as king, he ordered repairs to be done on God's Temple. The previous two administrations had not been kind to Solomon's Temple, and it hadn't really been given good maintenance since the time of King Hezekiah. There's a verse here giving Josiah's instructions: "But don't require the construction supervisors to keep account of the money they receive, for they are honest and trustworthy men" (2 Kings 22:7).

While repairing the Temple, the *Book of the Law* (most likely Deuteronomy, or perhaps the whole Torah) was found. We don't know how long it was missing, though I suspect it was gone at least as far as Manasseh's becoming king. It may have been longer. The people of God were continuing the rituals and practices but didn't have God's Word.

Josiah responded with horror when he heard the Word read and realized just how much his people have fallen. He heard the promises of what God would do if His people ignored His covenant, and he knew that sentence had already been carried out on the northern kingdom.

The people consulted the prophetess, Huldah. There were a number of women who spoke on God's behalf in the Old Testament. God calls who He will, and the people of Josiah's day had the good sense to recognize it. She sent a message to the king that, because of his repentance, God would hold off the coming disaster for another generation.

Josiah was also exposed to the early ministries of Jeremiah, Ezekiel, Nahum, Habakkuk, and Zephaniah. Despite knowing disaster awaited soon after his death, Josiah could look forward to a restoration of David's line in Jesus. The king who rediscovered the written Word heard about the coming of the incarnate Word:

> *"For my people will serve the Lord their God and their king descended from David—the king I will raise up for them"* (Jeremiah 30:9).

> *"The day is coming," says the Lord, "when I will make a new covenant with the people of Israel and Judah"* (Jeremiah 31:31).

He also heard how the arrival of Messiah would come at a terrible cost:

> *"This is what the Lord says: 'A cry is heard in Ramah—deep anguish and bitter weeping. Rachel weeps for her children, refusing to be comforted—for her children are gone'"* (Jeremiah 31:15).

Matthew points to this verse when he tells the story of Herod's slaughter of the infants, trying to eliminate the newborn King. But Zephaniah also prophesied of His coming, and the joy He would bring:

> *At last your troubles will be over, and you will never again fear disaster. On that day the announcement to Jerusalem will be, "Cheer up, Zion! Don't be afraid!* **For the Lord your God is living among you. He is a mighty savior.** *He will take delight in you with gladness. With his love, he will calm all your fears. He will rejoice over you with joyful songs"* (Zephaniah 3:15-17).

Consider: At Christmas, we sing songs celebrating the coming of our King. Let's not forget that He sings with joy for us, too.

December 12

JEHOIACHIN AND HIS BROTHERS

The Messiah Who makes a way despite human failure

After the exile to Babylon: Jehoiachin was the father of Shealtiel,

Once Josiah died, things swiftly went downhill. This is another case where Matthew's genealogy is compressing an ugly episode.

Jehoahaz "did what was evil in the Lord's sight" —lasted 3 months.

Eliakim "did what was evil in the Lord's sight" —lasted 11 years.

Jehoiachin "did what was evil in the Lord's sight" —lasted 8 years.

Zedekiah "did what was evil in the Lord's sight" —lasted 9 years.

Four kings in rapid succession, all evil, and the last died childless. There was another heir available, but he was taken to Babylon and never sat on the throne. No one else descended from Solomon sat on David's throne again.

Jeremiah had prophesied:

> "This is what the Lord says: 'Let the record show that this man Jehoiachin was childless. He is a failure, for none of his children will succeed him on the throne of David to rule over Judah'* (Jeremiah 22:29-30).

Jehoiachin was *not* childless. But from the perspective of royal succession, he might as well have been.

The Babylonians respected the royal line. Jehoiachin's heirs in Babylon were considered *Exilarchs*, that is, princes in exile. They were given special treatment and treated as nobility. They never actually ruled, but the line was still considered important, and continued to exist until about 1216 A.D., seeing the rise and fall of many empires, finally ending under Islamic rule.

So, if the Messiah was to be an heir of David, but the line was ended by Jeremiah's prophecy, now what?

This brings us back to David himself, and his moral failure with Bathsheba and the murder of Uriah, her husband. In 2 Samuel 12, the prophet Nathan confronted David about his sin. It was an incredibly gutsy move, considering the power David held. Rather than taking off Nathan's head, David, still sensitive to the Holy Spirit's conviction, repented. There were still consequences to deal with, but David remained "a man after God's own heart."

At some point later, David had another son that he named Nathan, probably after the man who had the courage to face the king and pull him back to the Lord. Nathan (the child) never ruled—that job belonged to his half-brother Solomon.

But Nathan was nevertheless a descendant of David, and so were his descendants. Luke later traced that line through Nathan to Christ, presumably through His mother, Mary.

While Jehoiachin and his relatives ended the list of Judah's rulers, the line went on to trace through to Joseph, Jesus' legal father. But God had another plan to put an heir of David on His throne, bypassing Jehoiachin by tracing through Nathan. He had set in place this plan hundreds of years before the failure of Judah's kings.

Jeremiah knew this, at least in part. For not only had he prophesied the end of the line for Judah's kings, but he also wrote:

> *"For the time is coming," says the Lord, "when I will raise up a righteous descendant from King David's line. He will be a King who rules with wisdom. He will do what is just and right throughout the land. And this will be his name: 'The LORD Is Our Righteousness'"* (Jeremiah 23:5-6).

His name invokes the covenant name of God, *YHWH*. (You can recognize this in most translations when you see LORD written in all capital letters.) So, this "descendant from David's line" will be both God and man.

The kingdom has ended. The King is coming.

Consider: Do you ever wonder how God will manage to make something good of a situation you're facing? Sometimes we may find that what we perceive as "plan B" was God's "plan A" all along. When life seems to collapse, He's still got you.

December 13

SHEALTIEL

The Messiah greater than empires

Shealtiel the father of Zerubbabel,

Just because the nation went into exile does not mean that prophecy suddenly came to an end. Several prophets spoke to the people in exile, while other prophesied in the era following the people's return.

Jeremiah predicted that the captivity would last 70 years (Jeremiah 29:10). This prediction is immediately followed by "For I know the plans I have for you," says the Lord. "They are plans for good and not for disaster, to give you a future and a hope" (verse 11).

Daniel 9:2 soon read, "During the first year of his reign, I, Daniel, learned from reading the word of the Lord, as revealed to Jeremiah the prophet, that Jerusalem must lie desolate for seventy years." So only a short time later, Jeremiah's prophecy is already considered "the word of the Lord."

Shealtiel was of that generation between the exile and the waves of returning exiles. The prophets gave his generation reason not only to look forward to the return to the Holy Land but look forward further to the coming of the Messiah.

Early in Daniel's ministry, he wrote about Nebuchadnezzar's dream of the great statue, depicting empires to come. You'll remember that Nebuchadnezzar was the one who invaded Judah and exiled the last king and people. He pictures the coming of Christ at the time of the Roman Empire like this:

> *As you watched, a rock was cut from a mountain, but not by human hands. It struck the feet of iron and clay, smashing them to bits. The whole statue*

was crushed into small pieces of iron, clay, bronze, silver, and gold. Then the wind blew them away without a trace, like chaff on a threshing floor. But the rock that knocked the statue down became a great mountain that covered the whole earth... During the reigns of those kings, the God of heaven will set up a kingdom that will never be destroyed or conquered. It will crush all these kingdoms into nothingness, and it will stand forever. That is the meaning of the rock cut from the mountain, though not by human hands, that crushed to pieces the statue of iron, bronze, clay, silver, and gold. The great God was showing the king what will happen in the future. The dream is true, and its meaning is certain. (Daniel 2:34-35,44-45).

Ezekiel around this same time pointed to Christ's coming in the context of "don't get your hopes up."

"Take off your jeweled crown, for the old order changes. Now the lowly will be exalted, and the mighty will be brought down. Destruction! Destruction! I will surely destroy the kingdom. And it will not be restored until the one appears who has the right to judge it. Then I will hand it over to him" (Ezekiel 21:26-27).

Ezekiel tells the people not to expect the kingdom to be restored until **the One** appears. And when Jesus comes, He preaches, "the Kingdom of God has arrived among you" (Luke 11:20).

Consider: In the midst of chaos and disaster, God still has a plan for you. His intent is that you will find hope in knowing there is a plan, while not necessarily knowing what the plan is.

December 14

ZERUBBABEL

The Messiah Who arrives right on schedule

Zerubbabel the father of Abihud,

Zerubbabel was allowed to return to Judah with 42,360 people (Ezra 2:64). But he did not return as king. Instead, under the rule of King Cyrus, who had conquered Babylon, Zerubbabel was authorized to act as *governor*. Things are not returning to the way they were before.

It was also around this time that the story of Shadrach, Meshach and Abednego, recorded in Daniel 3, shows the Jews' resistance to idol worship. It would seem the tendency to indulge in worshipping the idols of their neighbors was finally burned out of the Jewish psyche.

Daniel is still prophesying in Persia, even though some exiles have returned home. He told of Messiah this way:

> *"A period of seventy sets of seven has been decreed for your people and your holy city to finish their rebellion, to put an end to their sin, to atone for their guilt, to bring in everlasting righteousness, to confirm the prophetic vision, and to anoint the Most Holy Place. Now listen and understand! Seven sets of seven plus sixty-two sets of seven will pass from the time the command is given to rebuild Jerusalem until a ruler—the Anointed One—comes....*
>
> *"After this period of sixty-two sets of seven, the Anointed One will be killed, appearing to have accomplished nothing...* (Daniel 9:24-26).

There's a lot to unpack in this brief prophetic passage.

- Jesus is coming "to put an end to their sin, to atone for their guilt, to bring in everlasting righteousness, to confirm the prophetic vision, and to anoint the Most Holy Place." This is a clear picture of His death on the cross.

- His arrival was after seven sevens and sixty-two sevens, counting from the date Artaxerxes decreed that Jerusalem can be rebuilt. This decree was made on March 5, 445 B.C. 7x7 + 7x62 = 483.

Daniel is using prophetic years of 360 days rather than astronomical years of 365 ¼. John does this very thing in Revelation 11:2-3, idealizing a month as 30 days and a year as 360.

Now, if you take 483 years of 360 days apiece, you have 173,880 days. And 173,880 days after March 5, 445 BC is March 30, 33 AD.[1] This was the date that Moses commanded the Jews to take the Passover lamb into their homes (Exodus 12:3). This was the date that Jesus Christ rode into Jerusalem and was acclaimed as king. Today we know this day as Palm Sunday. Only a few days later the final Passover Lamb was sacrificed for the sins of the world.

Daniel is predicting *to the day* when Christ will come and be recognized as the Son of David and King of Israel, but shortly afterward was killed.

Zechariah, too, prophesied in Zerubbabel's day, saying:

> *Look, your king is coming to you. He is righteous and victorious, yet he is humble, riding on a donkey—riding on a donkey's colt* (Zechariah 9:9).

Zechariah 11 also indicates that at the time of Christ, the people would have unfit shepherds; that He would be rejected and hated; that He would be betrayed for thirty pieces of silver and the payment would be thrown into the Temple to buy the potter's field. Chapter 12 speaks of the people looking at the "One they had pierced."

---

[1] I'm using today's Gregorian calendar for all these dates for simplicity. Neither it nor the Julian calendar were in use anywhere in the Middle East on either of those dates.

The picture of the One to come is getting clearer and clearer. Even as Zerubbabel is working to rebuild the Temple, it is heard among the people that One is coming who will render the altar out of date and the building itself no longer necessary.

Consider: If God can work out the details of Jesus' arrival with such precision, can you believe He can work out the details in your life as well?

December 15

ABIUD

The Messiah who confronts and purifies

Abiud the father of Eliakim,

Zerubbabel didn't start a dynasty. Abiud didn't get to be governor after his father. In fact, he's not mentioned in the Old Testament at all. Zerubbabel was the last to be recorded; Matthew completed his genealogy using records outside the Hebrew Scriptures.

So, too, the prophetic record is coming to an end. By Abiud's generation, only the prophet Malachi is still speaking and writing.

"Look! I am sending my messenger, and he will prepare the way before me" (Malachi 3:1a).

Here Malachi is predicting the coming of John the Baptist, whom Jesus compared with Elijah. Malachi made the same comparison later in his book:

"Look, I am sending you the prophet Elijah before the great and dreadful day of the Lord arrives. His preaching will turn the hearts of fathers to their children, and the hearts of children to their fathers. Otherwise I will come and strike the land with a curse" (Malachi 4:5-6).

Jesus made the connection between Elijah and His cousin in Matthew 17:11-13:

"Jesus replied, 'To be sure, Elijah comes and will restore all things. But I tell you, Elijah has already come, and they did not recognize him, but have done to him everything they wished. In the same way the Son of Man is going to

suffer at their hands.' Then the disciples understood that he was talking to them about John the Baptist."

John's mission was to lay the groundwork for Christ's coming. He was to bring a message of repentance, for God's Kingdom was coming and was "at hand." Jesus, too, sometimes said God's Kingdom was coming, but other times said it had, in fact, arrived.

Speaking of Christ, Malachi pointed to Christ's mission to bring holiness of heart:

> *"He will sit like a refiner of silver, burning away the dross. He will purify the Levites, refining them like gold and silver, so that they may once again offer acceptable sacrifices to the Lord"* (Malachi 3:3).

Jesus, like John the Baptist, was particularly confrontational when dealing with the priests of his day, who were, of course, all Levites. All the Gospel accounts of these clashes ended with angry priests. But if you look forward a bit to Acts 6:7, we read that "God's message continued to spread. The number of believers greatly increased in Jerusalem, and many of the Jewish priests were converted, too." The work of Christ, coupled with the faithful testimony of His disciples after His ascension, fulfilled the prediction that Levites would be purified through faith in Him.

We also know that at least two members of the Jewish High Council, the Sanhedrin, believed in Him: Nicodemus and Joseph of Arimathea. Nicodemus spoke up in Jesus' defense (John 7:50-51). They both participated in Jesus' burial (John 19:38-39). These two were not necessarily Levites, but it is interesting to see how these two men risked their high positions and reputations to follow the Lord.

Messiah comes to purify and burn away that which is impure. Even some of His bitterest enemies came to believe.

Consider: Has Christ been trying to burn away any "dross" in your life? Is there anything you need to release to the Refiner's fire?

December 16

ELIAKIM

The Messiah Who conquers without a sword

> *Eliakim the father of Azor,*

By Eliakim's day the prophets have gone silent. The predictions Jesus would fulfill have all been written, and nothing more needed to be added. Some wrote other books, but the later Council of Jamnia in 90 A.D. settled the books of the Jewish Canon, excluding these other writings.

Protestants generally refer to these other writings as *The Apocrypha* (hidden writings) or *Pseudepigrapha* (false writings). But while they're not considered Scripture by Protestants, some of them provide important historical context.

Other ancient writers also offer help to understand what was going on between Malachi and Matthew. Josephus was a Jewish historian who offers a comprehensive history of the period. It's from these writings that we know that around the time of Eliakim, the Persian Empire that ruled over the Jews crumbled under the onslaught of the Greeks, led by Alexander the Great.

Alexander envisioned himself as ruler of the world. When he came to Jerusalem, according to Josephus,

> *...he [Alexander] went up into the temple, he offered sacrifice to God, according to the high priest's direction, and magnificently treated both the high priest and the priests. And when the Book of Daniel was showed him wherein Daniel declared that one of the Greeks should destroy the empire of the Persians, he supposed that himself was the person intended.*

Josephus conveniently leaves out the fact that Alexander is a Gentile and his presence in the Temple, offering a sacrifice, violates several points of Jewish law from the Torah. But what to do? He showed up with a *really* big army.

In Daniel 8, Persia had been pictured as a ram. But:

> *While I was watching, suddenly a male goat appeared from the west, crossing the land so swiftly that he didn't even touch the ground. This goat, which had one very large horn between its eyes, headed toward the two-horned ram that I had seen standing beside the river, rushing at him in a rage. The goat charged furiously at the ram and struck him, breaking off both his horns. Now the ram was helpless, and the goat knocked him down and trampled him. No one could rescue the ram from the goat's power. The goat became very powerful* (Daniel 8:5-8).

The angel Gabriel was dispatched to explain the vision to Daniel:

> *The shaggy male goat represents the king of Greece, and the large horn between his eyes represents the first king of the Greek Empire* (Daniel 8:21).

Alexander, who believed himself the destined ruler of the world, managed to put together an empire bigger than any that had come before. His conquests went as far as India. In June of 323 BC, he died in Nebuchadnezzar's palace, aged 32.

The title of eternal king of all the world belongs to Someone else. Someone who died at about the same age Alexander did—but refused to stay dead.

He couldn't have been more unlike Alexander. But He received everything Alexander so desperately craved:

> *Instead, he gave up his divine privileges; he took the humble position of a slave and was born as a human being. When he appeared in human form, he humbled himself in obedience to God and died a criminal's death on a cross.*
>
> *Therefore, God elevated him to the place of highest honor and gave him the name above all other names, that at the name of Jesus every knee should bow, in heaven and on earth and under the earth, and every tongue declare that Jesus Christ is Lord, to the glory of God the Father* (Philippians 2:7-11).

Consider: In your life you may face situations where you could try to force and bully your way to get what you want, or take the more humble approach, even giving up that which you have a right to. Honor Christ by doing it His way.

December 17

AZOR

The Messiah who defines our relationship to culture

Azor the father of Zadok,

Azor lived at the time after Alexander's conquests and death. The empire ended up being divided into four pieces, just as Daniel had predicted:

> *The goat became very powerful. But at the height of his power, his large horn was broken off. In the large horn's place grew four prominent horns pointing in the four directions of the earth* (Daniel 8:8).

The kingdom of Macedon controlled most of Greece (West). Pergamon controlled most of modern-day Turkey and Bulgaria (North). The Seleucid Empire got the largest territory, running from Syria to India (East), while the Ptolemaic kingdom took Egypt and the Sinai (South). It was these last two that concerned the people of Israel. The Jews were caught between these two empires, with Israel becoming the battleground.

The other issue Israel faced was that all the Greek empires felt that theirs was the highest, most perfect form of civilization, and it was their duty to "civilize" the places that they conquered. This meant spreading the Greek language, architecture, and culture across this vast domain. The widespread use of the Greek language later worked later to the advantage of Christianity, making it easier to spread over a huge area with no language barriers.

The Greeks in Israel insisted that their gods of Zeus, Hermes, Aphrodite, and so on be worshipped and have temples alongside the God of the Jews. Trade dramatically increased, with goods and people coming from much further away, exposing the people to more cultural influences.

Azor's people ended up faced with difficult choices—conform to the new cultural norms and generally prosper, or hold tight to the old ways and be left behind in the economic and social revolution.

Three centuries later, Jesus came preaching a message that encouraged His followers to be different than their surrounding culture yet have an influence on it. Jesus prayed:

> *"My prayer is not for the world, but for those you have given me, because they belong to you. .... Now I am departing from the world; they are staying in this world, but I am coming to you. ...*
>
> *"And the world hates them because they do not belong to the world, just as I do not belong to the world. I'm not asking you to take them out of the world, but to keep them safe from the evil one. They do not belong to this world any more than I do. Make them holy by your truth; teach them your word, which is truth.*
>
> *"I am praying not only for these disciples but also for all who will ever believe in me through their message. I pray that they will all be one, just as you and I are one—as you are in me, Father, and I am in you. And may they be in us so that the world will believe you sent me"* (John 17:6-21).

In the world but not of the world – connected enough to be an influence, but not so much as to be corrupted by it. That's what Christ called His people to.

He wouldn't want His people to be so isolated and afraid of the culture that they'd not have any way to make friends and share the gospel with their neighbors. But He also didn't want them to try so hard to be "relevant" that they'd end up being no different from the people they were trying to reach, making the gospel pointless and powerless.

Azor and his neighbors had to make a choice – be a Jew or be a Greek.

Consider: It's hard to strike a balance between living as part of a culture and allowing it to define your values, contrary to Christ's. How can you be "in" the world but not "of" it?

December 18

ZADOK

The Messiah Who loves "nobodies"

Zadok the father of Akim,

Zadok is surprisingly one of the most common names in the Bible. There were several people who had this name.

- At the time of Saul, David and Solomon there was a priest named Zadok who took the Ark of the Covenant into battle and acted as David's confidant throughout his rule.
- Another Zadok was King Jotham's father-in-law.
- There were at least two Zadoks at the time of Nehemiah's rebuilding of the walls of Jerusalem. One was the son of Baana, and the other the son of Immer. One of these Zadoks was a scribe, and Nehemiah 13:13 mentions him:

*"I assigned supervisors for the storerooms: Shelemiah the priest, **Zadok the scribe**, and Pedaiah, one of the Levites. And I appointed Hanan son of Zaccur and grandson of Mattaniah as their assistant. These men had an excellent reputation, and it was their job to make honest distributions to their fellow Levites."*

None of these men could have been the one from Matthew's genealogy. The scribe was a Levite, while the line of Christ runs through the tribe of Judah. As for the other Zadok, the father's name doesn't match. The timing also doesn't fit, as Nehemiah's rebuilding of Jerusalem is well over by this point.

If you're going to get your name in the Bible and can only get a quick mention—no exploits, no quotes, this is a great one. What an epitaph to have said of you, "excellent reputation…it was [his] job to make honest distributions." Auditors like me love to be able to report stuff like that.

But our Zadok isn't that other guy. We know nothing other than his name. It was a good name, an honorable name with a lot of history behind it.

We also know he lived at a time of increasing tensions between the Seleucids and the Ptolemies who ruled the Greek kingdoms surrounding Israel.

Perhaps we could think of him as a scriptural nobody. He might have been somebody in his day—we just don't know. Certainly, as far as the Bible is concerned, he was nobody famous.

But that's just it. Jesus had a thing for nobodies. We read a lot about Peter, James, John, even their mother, who I like to refer to as "Momma Thunder." But we don't get a lot about Nathaniel, Bartholomew, James the Lesser (known as "Little John" in television series *The Chosen*). Most of the twelve disciples get barely a mention in the Gospels or in Acts. We know where some of them were from, but they don't get a lot of lines in the Passion Plays.

Even the extrabiblical record doesn't give us much. They'll get a paragraph apiece in *Fox's Book of Martyrs*. You can read where they went and how they died—that's it. Scriptural nobodies.

Jesus called a *bunch* of nobodies. People who didn't need to get their greatest lines recorded. People who didn't obsess over getting the credit. These were just guys and gals who were called by the Master. They were sent two by two to proclaim the Kingdom. They were there when He said, "Go into the whole world and preach the gospel." And they did. They loved the Lord and served Him faithfully yet remained nobodies.

He came looking for people who understood that the moment you make it about you, it stops being about Him.

Consider: Wanna be a nobody? John the Baptist said, "He must become more, and I must become less." Learn to keep the focus off yourself and onto Jesus.

December 19   Akim

The Messiah without Whom we can do nothing

Akim the father of Elihud,

By Akim's day, the struggle between the Seleucids of Syria and territories east and the Ptolemies of Egypt and the south was coming to a head. The land is no longer called Judah but is now known as Judea, as the Romans later called it in Jesus' time.

King Antiochus, a Seleucid, decided to invade Egypt. The events around this time are recorded in the book of 2 Maccabees, which is one of those books that didn't make it into the canon of the Old Testament but still provides helpful historical background. Josephus' records are very similar, with a few extra details.

While Antiochus plows straight past Jerusalem on his way to his rival's capitol, rumors spread that the king is dead. The high priest, a man named Jason who had acquired the job through bribes, decided that this was his opportunity to throw off the rule of the Seleucids. He got a thousand men to follow him and attacked the Seleucid garrison in Jerusalem.

King Antiochus returned from Egypt, thinking the city was in revolt and he ordered a massacre of young and old. He went on to pillage God's Temple and slaughtered thousands. What went wrong? Jason must have wondered why God didn't side with him the way He had helped Joshua or Hezekiah win their battles. We don't know where Akim was in all this. Was he involved in the battle, or safely elsewhere in Judea?

Jason had repeated an error made throughout the Jews' time in the land: They thought God was on their side automatically. "If we fight to liberate the Temple, God will have to intervene!"

"If we carry the Ark of the Covenant into battle, we'll automatically win!" thought King Saul. The Philistines carried the Ark away.

At the time of Joshua, an angel met him before the invasion and Joshua asked, "Are you friend of foe?" "Neither one," he replied. "I am the commander of the Lord's army" (Joshua 5:13-14).

The question for Joshua isn't whether God and His angels are on his side. Joshua, are you on God's side?

Jason's leadership rested on corruption. He never asked his troops to consecrate themselves as Joshua had. God was almost an afterthought. He wasn't on God's side, so God wasn't on his. And the nation suffered for it.

Akim had the misfortune to live in times of war and devastation, brought on by people who were supposed to be serving God. There's an expression that's attributed to the Chinese that says, "May you live in interesting times." That's not a blessing.

Sometimes the circumstances of the day force us to see the distinction of more clearly being on God's side or not. I believe our nation, our world, is entering some of those "interesting times." Division and anger are rising to unfathomable levels.

The Messiah also came to live in "interesting times." There were zealots hoping to throw off Roman rule by force of arms. Jesus expected people to take sides, but not by picking up swords. Peter brandished a sword in the Garden of Gethsemane, but violence wasn't Jesus' way of doing things. He would, however, say, "Anyone who isn't with me opposes me, and anyone who isn't working with me is actually working against me" (Matthew 12:30).

Christ comes pleading, "Please don't get in My way, trying to win your battles with your plans using your resources. It doesn't work. Get on My side. Stop expecting God to pull *your* wagon. Instead, 'Take my yoke upon you. Let me teach you…'" (Matthew 11:29).

Consider: Are you seeking to align yourself with God's plans and purposes, or are you hoping God will get behind your plans?

December 20

Elihud

The Messiah Who comes as a light in darkness

Elihud the father of Eleazar,

Elihud is the Hannukah generation. Most of us know that Hannukah is a holiday that is on a different date each year, like Good Friday and Easter, because it's connected to the lunar calendar. It can start as early as November 28 or as late as December 26.

We're also looking at Elihud on December 20. The winter solstice falls each year either this day or the 21st. This means that tonight is probably the longest, darkest night of the year for readers in the northern hemisphere.

For Elihud, circumstances were pretty dark.

Antiochus IV, also called Epiphanes, rules the Seleucid Empire. He's had enough of Jewish refusals to cooperate with his efforts to become civilized in the image of Greek culture, and he's decided to stamp Judaism out once and for all. The Jews of the day nicknamed him, *Epimanes*, which means, "madman."

Second Maccabees continues the gruesome story. The Temple was renamed in honor of Zeus. It became a place of drunkenness and prostitution. People were forbidden to keep the Sabbath, Jewish festivals, or even call themselves Jews.

King Antiochus held a birthday celebration once a month and ordered pigs to be sacrificed on the Lord's altar to Dionysius, god of wine. Jews were expected to share in the sacrificial meat and participate in the drunken festivities. Those who refused were tortured and killed.

Along came another rebel, Judas Maccabeus, wiser than Jason. He starts his revolution with prayer and seeks God's mercy and guidance. Judas encouraged his followers, "'For they trust to arms and acts of daring...but we trust in the Almighty God, who is able with a single nod to strike down those who are coming against us, and even, if necessary, the whole world.' Moreover, he told them of the occasions when help came to their ancestors..." He appointed a man named Eleazar to read from God's Word to encourage the soldiers. Faith was the fuel that ran this revolution.

The stories of Judas Maccabeus' battles are filled with phrases like, "with the Lord as an ally," and "with the help of the Lord." They defeated their enemies again and again. A desperate King Antiochus rode to the final battle:

> *In his arrogance he said, "When I get there, I will make Jerusalem a cemetery of Jews." But the all-seeing Lord, the God of Israel, struck him with an incurable and invisible blow...*

Judas Maccabeus and his followers went on to tear down all the pagan modifications to the Temple, rebuild the altar and purify the Holy Place. They celebrated God's goodness with an eight-day celebration, which became the annual Festival of Lights or Hannukah, because God miraculously allowed their limited supply of ceremonial oil to last for eight nights.

Dark times led to the Festival of Lights. And on this darkest of nights of the year, we remember that because of Jesus,

> *The light shines in the darkness, and the darkness can never extinguish it* (John 1:5).

> *The people who sat in darkness have seen a great light. And for those who lived in the land where death casts its shadow, a light has shined* (Matthew 4:16)

> *I am the light of the world. If you follow me, you won't have to walk in darkness, because you will have the light that leads to life* (John 8:12).

> *For the darkness is disappearing, and the true light is already shining* (1 John 2:8).

Consider: When times are dark, remember that Christ's light can never be put out. When you put your trust in Him, your resources always last longer than you think they will.

ELIHUD

When we have exhausted our store of endurance,
When our strength has failed ere the day is half done,
When we reach the end of our hoarded resources
Our Father's full giving is only begun.

— Annie J. Flint

December 21

ELEAZAR

The Messiah Who confounded the wise

Eleazar the father of Matthan,

It was at this time that the Greek powers have collapsed and Judea had a time of relative peace, and much of the credit goes to a high priest named John Hyrcanus. To the west a new power has emerged—Rome.

Hyrcanus is a Pharisee—and the minority party is the Sadducees—the very same two parties that were thorns in Jesus' side. The Pharisees emphasized a strict reading of the Holy Scriptures and took the text literally as much as they could. This group held sway over most common people.

The rival party, the Sadducees, were primarily the party of the wealthy and powerful, and preferred a looser interpretation of the biblical texts. They believed in unrestricted free will—that God didn't really care about human behavior. The only exception was issues of ritual purity, which allowed them to keep running the Temple and keep the shekels flowing into their coffers.

> *[Hyrcanus] once invited them to a feast and entertained them very kindly, and when he saw them in a good humor... he requested, that if they observed him offending in any point and straying from the right way, they should call him back and correct him. On that occasion they attested to his being entirely virtuous, and with this commendation he was very pleased.* (Josephus' Antiquities, XIII, 288-290)

Here John Hyrcanus is falling into a trap of pride in his own righteousness, and his Pharisee comrades are setting him up.

> *But there was one of his guests there whose name was Eleazar, a man of evil nature, who delighted in seditious practices. This man said, "Since you desire to know the truth, if you are righteous in earnest, give up the high priesthood and content yourself with the civil government of the people… We have heard it from the elders that your mother had been a captive during the reign of Antiochus Epiphanes." This story was false, and Hyrcanus was furious with him, and all the Pharisees were very indignant against him. (vv. 291-292)*

The implication here is that "your mother got pregnant with you while she was held prisoner by Antiochus Epiphanes. You're the illegitimate son of that awful king who ruined our Temple." Or at the very least, "your mother wasn't a virgin when she got married," which would have disqualified him from the priesthood under Leviticus 21:13-14.

Hyrcanus went into a terrible rage at this defamation of his character. He ended up switching parties and joined the Sadducees. By Jesus' day, the high priests Annas and Caiaphas were both Sadducees.

The infighting between the two parties was still going strong in Jesus' day. In Matthew 22, the Sadducees tried to trip Him up with a question about a woman being successively married to seven brothers who had each, in turn, died.

> *"So tell us, whose wife will she be in the resurrection? For all seven were married to her." Jesus replied, "Your mistake is that you don't know the Scriptures, and you don't know the power of God." (vv. 28-29)*

At this point the Pharisees see an opportunity. Not only could they trap Jesus with His words, but they could also kick their rivals while they were down.

> *But when the Pharisees heard that he had silenced the Sadducees with his reply, they met together to question him again. (v. 34)*

But His answers stumped the Pharisees as well. The coming Messiah confounded both Sadducees and Pharisees, and they both hated Him for it. Extinguishing this threat to their power moved them to a rare moment of cooperation.

Jesus wasn't about law, but about grace. The Pharisees couldn't get it. But He also emphasized that human behavior, especially how we treat our neighbors, matters to God. So, the Sadducees couldn't fathom Him, either.

The Christ was bringing something new that wouldn't stay in the old wineskins. Imagine if they knew He would arrive in a stable!

Consider: Do you align yourself with groups, denominations and parties to the extent that there's no room in your faith for Christ to do the unexpected?

December 22

MATTHAN

The Messiah who warns against power seeking

Matthan the father of Jacob,

The power struggles within Judea's Sanhedrin are, of course, not unique to that part of the world. Jockeying for power is a universal constant.

By Matthan's generation, one such power struggle is about to transform the Roman Republic into the Roman Empire. Three men—Julius Caesar, Crassus and Pompey—have formed a group they call the Triumvirate to try to consolidate power in the fracturing republic.

These three men had mixed motives – to get the Republic functioning would have been a good thing, but they also coveted power for themselves. And if those two values came into conflict, power always trumped virtue.

Caesar and Pompey both went on military campaigns to bring themselves more honor in the Senate.

Caesar entered Rome with his military fully armed, and in a brief civil war, took over as undisputed dictator. His last name, Caesar, became a title for future all-powerful leaders.

Julius Caesar thought so highly of himself that he designed a new calendar, named a month after himself, and then stole a day from February to add to July since his month deserved to be the biggest. His successor, Augustus, would do the same thing, leaving poor February with only 28 days.

Only a few short years later, Julius was assassinated in the Senate by two of his trusted friends.

This devolution of the Roman Republic into a dictatorship was one of many pieces God was going to use to prepare the world for the coming of Christ. Jesus Messiah came soon afterward, warning of the dangers of the accumulation of power. I've already mentioned earlier that the mother of James and John sought positions for her sons and didn't really like the answer she got. But the reaction of the other ten disciples is also problematic. They were indignant, which is an emotion that betrays the fact that they weren't just mad that James and John used their mother for a powerplay. Perhaps they were mad they didn't think to make the powerplay first.

> *So Jesus called them together and said, "You know that the rulers in this world lord it over their people, and officials flaunt their authority over those under them. But among you it will be different. Whoever wants to be a leader among you must be your servant, and whoever wants to be first among you must be the slave of everyone else. For even the Son of Man came not to be served but to serve others and to give his life as a ransom for many"* (Mark 10:42-45).

Jesus' warning is not just directed to James, John, and Momma Thunder. He's talking to the whole group. Every disciple of Christ must guard themselves against the accumulation of power unto themselves.

Christ Himself modelled this. His whole life was about the dissipation of personal power. He gave up the majesty of the Godhead to become human and continued to release Himself from power to become a servant. Finally, He submitted to death on a cross, even though He could have called upon legions of angels to release Him from that fate. People recognized that He had personal authority, but He never used it for His own benefit or at the expense of others.

He comes among us as One who serves.

Consider: In what ways does the temptation for personal position and power manifest itself in your life? How can you tamp that down?

December 23

JACOB

The Messiah who approves of taxation

and Jacob the father of Joseph

In 79 B.C., Pompey invaded Judea and made it a Roman province. Jacob, Jesus' grandfather, was the first generation to live under Roman hegemony. Rome installed garrisons to maintain order and squelch any uprisings. Jewish zealots constantly plotted the rebellion that failed again and again.

Roman rule also required a lot of money, and the Romans were very good at taxation. Matthew would eventually be a tax collector for the Empire. He was hated for it by his own people.

The weak Hasmonean kings that had briefly ruled fell out of power. They never really had the power of kings anyway; that belonged to the high priest and Sanhedrin. Rome eventually installed another line of puppet kings more pleasing to the Empire: the Herods, who were not Jewish but rather were from a place the Romans called *Idumea*. The Old Testament calls this land *Edom*. Thus, in addition to being under Rome's thumb, the Jews suffered the indignity of having to call a man from Edom their "king."

When Jesus came, He was very early on considered the friend of tax collectors. He didn't view anyone as unredeemable, so long as they were willing to believe in Him. He specifically went looking for this sort of people.

That doesn't mean He was okay with the practices of oppressive tax collectors who used their position to abuse people. "Even corrupt tax collectors came to be baptized and asked, 'Teacher, what should we do?' He replied, 'Collect no more taxes than the government requires'" (Luke 3:12-13). So, Jesus wasn't against taxes, just abusive tax practices. Jesus' forgiveness and holiness led Zacchaeus to volunteer, "I will give half my wealth to the poor, Lord, and if I have cheated people on their taxes, I will give them back four times as much!"

Jesus' enemies tried to trap him with questions of taxation, but He told them, "give to Caesar what belongs to Caesar, and give to God what belongs to God." (Luke 20:25)

Jesus knew how corrupt the Roman government could be and where much of the tax money ended up. Nevertheless, He defended the legitimacy of the government collecting the tax.

Jesus also defended the practice in His day of a tax to support the Temple.

> *On their arrival in Capernaum, the collectors of the Temple tax came to Peter and asked him, "Doesn't your teacher pay the Temple tax?" "Yes, he does," Peter replied. Then he went into the house. But before he had a chance to speak, Jesus asked him, "What do you think, Peter? Do kings tax their own people or the people they have conquered?" "They tax the people they have conquered," Peter replied.*
>
> *"Well, then," Jesus said, "the citizens are free! However, we don't want to offend them, so go down to the lake and throw in a line. Open the mouth of the first fish you catch, and you will find a large silver coin. Take it and pay the tax for both of us."*

It's interesting to note that Peter brought up a religious tax imposed by the Jews, while it looks like Jesus' answer is addressing the Roman government taxation. Perhaps He was subtly commenting on the level of cozy relationship between the Sanhedrin and Roman leadership – one tax is pretty much like the other.

Jacob lived in the day when the Romans started to tax Judea into poverty, and by Jesus' day it was no less oppressive. All the same, Jesus did not come to get rid of the taxman. He wanted good redemption, not good riddance.

Consider: Do you pay all the tax that you owe? What about what you owe to God through tithes and offerings? It's not about legalism; it's about giving from a grateful heart.

December 24

JOSEPH

The Messiah who simply does what is right

Joseph, the husband of Mary, and Mary was the mother of Jesus

For Christmas Eve we come to Joseph. Here is a man the New Testament tells us a few things about.

Matthew's Gospel picks up right after the genealogy:

> *This is how Jesus the Messiah was born. His mother, Mary, was engaged to be married to Joseph. But before the marriage took place, while she was still a virgin, she became pregnant through the power of the Holy Spirit. Joseph, to whom she was engaged, was a righteous man and did not want to disgrace her publicly, so he decided to break the engagement quietly.*
>
> *As he considered this, an angel of the Lord appeared to him in a dream. "Joseph, son of David," the angel said, "do not be afraid to take Mary as your wife. For the child within her was conceived by the Holy Spirit. And she will have a son, and you are to name him Jesus, for he will save his people from their sins."*
>
> *All of this occurred to fulfill the Lord's message through his prophet: "Look! The virgin will conceive a child! She will give birth to a son, and they will call him Immanuel, which means 'God is with us.'"*
>
> *When Joseph woke up, he did as the angel of the Lord commanded and took Mary as his wife. But he did not have sexual relations with her until her son was born. And Joseph named him Jesus* (Matthew 1:18-25).

Luke also tells us that Mary "was engaged to be married to a man named Joseph, a descendant of King David" (Luke 1:27). "And because Joseph was a descendant of King David, he had to go to Bethlehem in Judea, David's ancient home [for the census]. He traveled there from the village of Nazareth in Galilee" (Luke 2:4).

Joseph is further mentioned as being present when the shepherds showed up in the middle of the night, and in the narrative of Jesus' presentation at the Temple eight days later. He received messages from God in dreams at least twice—once telling him to get married, and the other to leave town in a hurry.

In several other places in the Gospels, we hear that Joseph was a carpenter.

What we know of the culture of Joseph's day was that he was probably at least 30 years old when he married, and his bride would have been substantially younger. Church tradition says he was probably older than that. This age difference may help explain why Mary seems to have outlived her husband.

What do we really know about this man entrusted to care for God's Son?

Here's a few takeaways:

- He was described as a "righteous man," so he cared about the things that matter to God. But in the same sentence it says that he did not want to publicly disgrace Mary for her out-of-wedlock pregnancy, even though the law required her to be stoned. Here's a man who is more about the principles of righteousness and less about the letter of the law. I think Joseph would have been very comfortable with the New Testament concept of *grace*.

- Joseph is the kind of man who, when he receives a message from God, has no need to wrestle, ponder or otherwise delay. He just does what the Lord asks.

- He's just a simple working man. Descended from kings and governors, there doesn't seem to be a shred of pretentiousness on him. He's just a hard-working, blue-collar guy. He's exactly the kind of man that Jesus would one day choose for disciples.

Consider: How can you be righteous without being legalistic? How can you extend grace to those you interact with who are in situations that look bad?

December 25

JESUS

The One called the Messiah

Jesus who is called the Messiah

Today is the day the Western Church celebrates the coming of Jesus Christ into the world. The fulfillment of centuries of prophecy has led to this, and it is right that we have a day to annually remember Jesus' coming as a child. The Son of God went through the experience of being born and growing up. "This high priest of ours understands our weaknesses, for he faced all of the same testings we do, yet he did not sin" (Hebrews 4:15).

There are at least 200 specific prophecies in the Old Testament that point to the coming of Christ. But only a couple talked about Christmas. That's about one percent.

One was Micah 5:2: "But you, O Bethlehem Ephrathah, are only a small village among all the people of Judah. Yet a ruler of Israel, whose origins are in the distant past, will come from you on my behalf." Herod's advisors heard this quote when the Magi showed up asking, "Where is He?"

One other was Jeremiah 31:15, "A cry is heard in Ramah— deep anguish and bitter weeping. Rachel weeps for her children, refusing to be comforted— for her children are gone." Matthew refers to this verse in the context of Herod's slaughter of the children of Bethlehem and surrounding territory.

But there's one more that many people miss. Matthew 2:23 says, "So the family went and lived in a town called Nazareth. This fulfilled what the prophets had said:

'He will be called a Nazarene.'" Yes, Jesus is at least a toddler by this point, but He's still a young child so I count it in with Christmas.

If you look in a Bible that adds footnotes when the New Testament quotes an Old Testament verse, there isn't a footnote for Matthew 2:23. "He will be called a Nazarene" does not show up, word for word, anywhere in the Old Testament. So why did Matthew say this was a fulfillment of prophecy? Didn't anyone in seminary teach him to cite his references?

I think Matthew is referring to Isaiah 11:1:

> *Out of the stump of David's family will grow a shoot—yes, a new **Branch** bearing fruit from the old root.*

"Branch" in Hebrew is רֵצַן, pronounced "netser." So, Nazareth is the "place of the Branch." Over the centuries since Isaiah wrote about the Branch from David's stump, the little "branch town" in Galilee came to be associated with the Branch to come. Some thought nothing good could come from there (John 1:46), but others knew.

Two Christmas prophecies – three if you count the "netser" reference. That's it. Ninety-nine percent of the prophecies deal with Christ as an adult or as the returning, triumphant King. Why so little?

Christmas gifts are more fun when there's a surprise. Sometimes God doesn't reveal everything. He has wonderful mysteries yet to uncover. He never mentioned to any of the Old Testament prophets a word about the stable, the shepherds, the angels, or the Magi. *He left some wonders unforetold.*

Each year we read again the narratives of Matthew and Luke; we sing the familiar carols and light the advent wreath once more. It never gets old, because while we've heard it all before, there are still some wonders for Him to reveal to our hearts.

This Christmas, find that unrevealed wonder God has yet to show you. "Let's see this thing that has happened, which the Lord has told us about" (Luke 2:15).

Consider: Amongst the celebrations of today, ask the Lord of Christmas to show you something new.

About the Author

Major Stephen M. Kelly, along with his wife, Major Leanne, were commissioned in the *Messengers of Peace* session in 1987 in The Salvation Army USA Eastern Territory. They served 16 years as corps officers in six states. Major Stephen served in finance in the Massachusetts, Western Pennsylvania and Southwest Ohio divisions, after which they were appointed to the USA Eastern Territory Audit Department. In 2019 they came to the USA Southern Territory, where together they led the Southern Territory Audit Department. In 2023, the Kellys moved on to financial roles in the Southwest Ohio & Northeast Kentucky division.

www.ingramcontent.com/pod-product-compliance
Lightning Source LLC
Chambersburg PA
CBHW081016040426
42444CB00014B/3234